Kentucky

College Basketball

NAMES
&
GAMES

Manufactured in the United States of America
Cover design and book layout by James Asher Graphics

Other titles from McClanahan Publishing House, Inc.

Crazy About the Cats, From Rupp to Pitino
Dining in Historic Kentucky
Dining in Historic Georgia
Dining in the Historic South
Savor Lake Superior
Nuts About Pecans
On Bended Knees: The Night Rider Story
Kentucky's Thomas D. Clark
Cooking With Curtis Grace
Cook Talk With Curtis Grace and Friends
A Little Touch of Grace

McClanahan
Publishing House

All book correspondence should be addressed to:
McClanahan Publishing House, Incorporated
P.O. Box 100
Kuttawa, Kentucky 42055

(502) 388 9388
1 800 544 6959

FEATURING

University of Kentucky
University of Louisville
Western Kentucky University
Eastern Kentucky University
Murray State University
Morehead State University
Kentucky State University
Kentucky Wesleyan College
Bellarmine College
Georgetown College
Campbellsville College
Lindsey Wilson College
Northern Kentucky University
Paducah Community College
Transylvania
Centre College

Kentucky
College Basketball
NAMES
&
GAMES

Compiled by Jim Pickens, Jr.

McClanahan
Publishing House

ACKNOWLEDGEMENTS

An endeavor such as this would not have been possible without the tireless efforts of many individuals, past and present, who have made significant contributions to the storied history of college basketball in Kentucky.

First and foremost, a hearty salute goes out to the state's university and college sports information directors and their staffs, an often-underappreciated lot who were the first to document many of the facts and figures contained herein. Great appreciation is also extended to the long list of distinguished journalists who have not only reported the action but who, in many instances, have helped define the essence of the state's most consistently popular sport.

Finally, a slam-dunk thank you to the players, coaches, fans and all others associated with the game, who in the course of the 20th century have made college basketball in Kentucky a treasure of unforgettable memories.

DEDICATION

This book is dedicated to the memories and acheivements of Ed Diddle and Adolph Rupp, a colorful pair of orginal masters who laid the foundation for it all; and to the memory of Bud Tyler, a dear friend.

J.E.P.

September, 1993

TABLE OF CONTENTS

CHAPTER 1

NAMES

Q. What was the original name of the Metro Conference?
A. Metro Six (charter teams were Louisville, Memphis State, Cincinnati, Georgia Tech, St. Louis and Tulane)

Q. What nickname was accorded Kentucky point guard Travis Ford during the 1992-93 season?
A. "The Little General"

Q. What former Kentucky and Morehead State player was the 20th-ranked scorer in NAIA Division I in 1992-93?
A. Jody Thompson (20.2 points per game for Pikeville College)

Q. What was the Louisville basketball team dubbed during World War II?
A. "Sea Cards" (all of the players were in the Navy)

Q. What was the first name of 1920s Western Kentucky star "Pap" Glenn?
A. Harry

Q. Who is the veteran public address announcer for Louisville home games?
A. John Tong

Q. What was the nickname of UK's Phil Grawemeyer?
A. "Cookie"

Q. What Murray State player was a second round selection by the Houston Rockets in the 1992 NBA Draft?
A. Popeye Jones

Q. Who led UK in free throw shooting in 1991-92?
A. Gimel Martinez (88.3 percent, 68 of 77)

Q. Who has been broadcasting Western Kentucky games since 1964-65?
A. Wes Strader

Q. What was the nickname of 1920s Louisville coach C.V. Money?
A. "Red"

Q. Who were UK's first non-manager coaches?
A. R.E. Spahr and E.R. Sweetland (1909-10)

Q. What is Lindsey Wilson College's nickname?
A. "Blue Raiders"

Q. What was the nickname of UK standout Layton Rouse?
A. "Mickey"

Q. What Morehead State star was later a big-league pitcher for 11 seasons with the New York Yankees, Washington Senators, Cleveland Indians, Chicago White Sox, Chicago Cubs and San Francisco Giants?
A. Steve Hamilton

Q. What is the nickname of Louisville coach Denny Crum?
A. "Cool Hand Luke"

Q. Who led Kentucky in scoring in the Wildcats' 1993 NCAA Tournament victory over Florida State?
A. Jared Prickett (22 points)

Q. Who led Murray State in scoring during the 1973-74 season?
A. Mike Coleman (24.1 points per game)

Q. What was the nickname of Louisville's Pervis Ellison?
A. "Never Nervous"

Q. Who was the leading scorer on UK's 1967-68 team?
A. Mike Casey (20.1 points per game)

Q. In John Oldham's first season as coach at Western Kentucky (1964-65), who were his two full-time assistants?
A. Gene Rhodes and Buck Sydnor

Q. Who is the only Louisville player to finish his career with an average of over 20 points per game?
A. Wes Unseld (20.6, 1966-68)

Q. What was the nickname of Western Kentucky's high-flying forward, Tony Wilson?
A. "TWA"

Q. What current coach of a state team was captain of Evansville's NCAA Division II championship team of 1964?
A. Wayne Boultinghouse (of Kentucky Wesleyan)

Q. Who was Eastern Kentucky's first coach?
A. Clyde H. Wilson (1909-10; 3-3 record)

Q. Who was the starting center on Joe B. Hall's first UK team, 1971-72?
A. Jim Andrews

Q. What was the nickname of UK's Cotton Nash?
A. "King Cotton"

Q. What former Murray State star once scored 62 points in an American Basketball Association game?
A. Stew Johnson (vs. Jacksonville Floridians, 1971)

Q. What Louisville star was a first-round NBA draft choice of the Atlanta Hawks in 1969?
A. Butch Beard

Q. What was the nickname of Western Kentucky's Clem Haskins?
A. "The Gem"

Q. What UK All-American was a native of Lebanon, Pa.?
A. Sam Bowie

Q. What guard led Murray State in free throw percentage three consecutive seasons, 1968-71?
A. Jimmy Young

Q. What former Louisville star holds the school's outdoor discus record in track and field?
A. Wes Unseld

Q. Who played center for UK's "Rupp's Runts" during the 1965-66 season?
A. Thad Jaracz (6-feet-5)

Q. Who was the first Morehead State player on record to record over 100 assists in a season?
A. Bobby Hiles (162, 1969-70)

Q. What was the nickname of 1940s Western Kentucky star Howard Downing?
A. "Tip"

Q. What player led Denny Crum's first Louisville team in scoring, 1971-72?
A. Jim Price (21 points per game)

Q. What did UK coach Adolph Rupp dub his three sophomores, Larry Conley, Tommy Kron and Micky Gibson, during the 1963-64 season?
A. "Katzenjammer Kids"

Q. Who followed Wayne Martin as Morehead State coach in 1987?
A. Tommy Gaither

Q. What was the name of Clem Haskins' younger brother, who played at Western Kentucky from 1968-70?
A. Paul Haskins

Q. What former Vanderbilt play-by-play broadcaster became color analyst for the UK Basketball Network in 1992?
A. Charlie McAlexander

Q. Who led Louisville in rebound average in 1959-60?
A. Fred Sawyer (14.1 per game)

Q. What was the nickname of UK's Dan Issel?
A. "The Horse"

Q. Who were the starting guards on Peck Hickman's final Louisville team, 1966-67?
A. Fred Holden and Dave Gilbert

Q. What UK assistant coach helped lead Rick Pitino's 1987 Providence team to the Final Four?
A. Billy Donovan

Q. Who led Louisville's first basketball team in scoring, 1911-12?

A. C. N. Caldwell (5.3 points per game)

Q. Other than Steve Hamilton, who is the only Morehead State player to accumulate 1,000 rebounds?

A. Norm Pokey (1,046, 1960-63)

Q. What was the nickname of 1920s Louisville guard Ed Craddock?

A. "Froggy"

Q. Who is the radio play-by-play broadcaster for Louisville games?

A. Van Vance

Q. Who was the first UK player to score 40 points in a game?

A. Bill Spivey (40, vs. Georgia Tech, 1950)

Q. Who followed Robert Wilson as Kentucky Wesleyan coach in 1959?

A. T. L. Plain

Q. What Morehead State star of the '60s was nicknamed "Hobo"?

A. Willie Jackson

Q. Following his 1964 retirement, who did former Western Kentucky coach Ed Diddle call the best all-around athlete he coached in 42 seasons at the school?
A. Harry "Pap" Glenn (who captained Western's basketball, football and baseball teams in 1925)

Q. What was the starting lineup of UK's first team in 1903?
A. J. White Guyn, R. H. Arnett (guards), H. J. Wurtele, Lee Andrews (forwards), Joe Coons (center)

Q. Who coached Georgetown College to the national championship game of the 1961 NAIA Tournament?
A. Bob Davis

Q. Who was Morehead State's first coach?
A. George Downing (1929-30; 9-3 record)

Q. Who led Louisville in scoring in 1962?
A. Bud Olsen (20.8 points per game)

Q. Who became Louisville's first 1,000-point scorer in 1949?
A. Jack Coleman (finished with 1,114 points)

Q. What was the nickname of Western Kentucky star guard Forest Able?
A. "Frosty"

Q. Who led UK in field goal percentage three consecutive seasons, 1956-58?
A. Vernon Hatton

Q. What was the nickname of UK All-American Jamal Mashburn?
A. "Monster Mash"

Q. Who was the first Kentucky Wesleyan player to play in the NBA?
A. Virgil Vaughn (Boston Celtics, 1946-47, Syracuse Nationals, 1947-48)

Q. Who made eight three-point baskets in a game three times for UK in 1989-90?
A. Derrick Miller

Q. Who was the only Wildcat to average double-figures in scoring during UK's NIT championship season of 1946?
A. Jack Parkinson (11.3 points per game)

Q. What is Northern Kentucky University's nickname?
A. "Norse"

Q. Who led Morehead State in scoring in 1970 and '71?
A. Jim Day (22.0 in '70; 24.1 in '71)

Q. What father of a 1992-93 UK starter played at Murray State from 1963-66?
A. Eddie Ford (father of Travis Ford)

Q. Who was the leading scorer for Louisville during the team's Final Four season of 1975?
A. Allen Murphy (16.3 points per game)

Q. Who led Western Kentucky in scoring during John Oldham's first season as coach, 1964-65?
A. Clem Haskins (23.4 points per game)

Q. Who was UK's first African-American player?
A. Tom Payne (1970-71)

Q. What former Western Kentucky player was the first coach of the ABA's Kentucky Colonels?
A. Johnny Givens (1967)

Q. What Morehead State guard averaged 23.6 points per game to lead the Eagles to the 1961 Ohio Valley Conference championship?
A. Granville Williams

Q. Who did Adolph Rupp claim was the strongest player he coached in 41 seasons at Kentucky?
A. LeRoy Edwards

Q. What player-turned-broadcaster led UK in assists three consecutive seasons, 1964-66?
A. Larry Conley

Q. What Western Kentucky star was killed in an auto accident following his senior season in 1967?
A. Dwight Smith

Q. What All-American center led Western Kentucky to its only Final Four appearance in 1971?
A. Jim McDaniels

Q. Who led Murray State in free throw percentage in 1992?
A. Cedric Gumm (.827, 62 of 75)

Q. What UK fan had attended 511 consecutive Wildcat basketball games entering the 1993-94 season?
A. Bob Wiggins (last missed a game in 1977)

Q. Before changing it to "Colonels" in the 1960s, what was Eastern Kentucky's nickname?
A. "Maroons"

Q. Who was the 7-feet-1 center who helped lead Kentucky State to NAIA championships in 1970 and '71?
A. Elmore Smith

Q. What Murray State guard made 19 free throws in a game three times in his career?
A. Howie Crittenden

Q. Who coached Kentucky Wesleyan to its first NCAA Division II championship in 1966?
A. Guy Strong

Q. What Western Kentucky player was the Boston Celtics' number one draft choice in 1971?
A. Clarence Glover

Q. What Mississippi State transfer led Murray State in scoring and rebounding in 1979-80?
A. Gary Hooker

Q. Who coaches Pikeville College?
A. Rick Scruggs

Q. The Ohio Valley Conference, formed in 1948, featured what five Kentucky schools as charter members?
A. Western, Eastern, Morehead, Murray, Louisville (the other charter member was Evansville)

Q. What Murray State and NBA Hall of Famer was nicknamed "Jumpin' Joe"?
A. Joe Fulks

Q. What UK player was selected in the sixth round of the 1972 NBA Draft by the Cleveland Cavaliers?
A. Tom Parker

Q. Who was the first Western Kentucky player to reach the 1,000-rebounds mark?
A. Tom Marshall (1954, finished with 1,225)

Q. What Eastern Kentucky guard was second in the nation in scoring in 1945?
A. Fred Lewis (22.1 points per game)

Q. Who were the starting guards on UK's 1958 NCAA champions?
A. Vernon Hatton and Adrian Smith

Q. What forward led Murray State in scoring in 1972 and '73?
A. Les Taylor (25.6 ppg in '72; 22.4 ppg in '73)

Q. Who followed Paul McBrayer as Eastern Kentucky coach in 1962?
A. Jim Beachtold

Q. Who was the starting center on Denny Crum's first Louisville team, 1971-72?
A. Al Vilcheck

Q. What is the first name of former Louisville star "Junior" Bridgeman?
A. Ulysses

Q. What moniker was accorded UK seniors Richie Farmer, Deron Feldhaus, John Pelphrey and Sean Woods following the 1991-92 season?
A. "The Unforgettables"

Q. What former Western Kentucky player coached Kentucky Wesleyan to NCAA Division II championships in 1968 and '69?
A. Bob Daniels

Q. Who led Morehead State in scoring and rebounding during the 1975-76 season?
A. Ted Hundley (18.8 ppg, 10.9 rpg)

Q. Who were Kentucky's "Fabulous Five" of 1948?
A. Alex Groza (center), Ralph Beard and Kenny Rollins (guards), "Wah Wah" Jones and Cliff Barker (forwards)

Q. What guard led UK in free throw percentage in 1971?
A. Kent Hollenbeck (88.2)

Q. What was the nickname of Western Kentucky All-American Don Ray?
A. "Duck"

Q. Who coached Kentucky Wesleyan to NCAA Division II championships in 1987 and '90?
A. Wayne Chapman

Q. What was the nickname of Eastern Kentucky star James Tillman?
A. "Turk"

Q. Who preceeded Adolph Rupp as UK coach?
A. John Mauer

Q. Who coached Eastern Kentucky to the 1972 OVC championship?
A. Guy Strong

Q. Who followed John Oldham as Western Kentucky coach in 1971?
A. Jim Richards

Q. What was the nickname of Louisville's Milt Wagner?
A. "Ice"

Q. Who coached Kentucky State to three consecutive NAIA championships, 1970-72?
A. Lucias Mitchell

Q. Who coaches Campbellsville College?
A. Lou Cunningham

Q. Who led UK in assists three consecutive seasons, 1981-83?
A. Dirk Minniefield

Q. What member of Western Kentucky's 1971 Final Four team was nicknamed "Big C"?
A. Clarence Glover

Q. Who is second on the career rebounding list at Kentucky?
A. Frank Ramsey (1,038)

Q. Who followed Ellis Johnson as Morehead State coach in 1953?
A. Bobby Laughlin

Q. Who was the starting point guard on Louisville's 1975 Final Four team?
A. Phillip Bond

Q. Who led UK in scoring in 1975?
A. Kevin Grevey (23.6 points per game)

Q. Who served as Louisville's interim coach after John Dromo suffered a heart attack during the 1970-71 season?
A. Howard Stacey (12-8 record)

Q. Who coached Murray State from 1954-58?
A. Rex Alexander

Q. Who was Louisville's starting center from 1975-78?
A. Ricky Gallon

Q. What does the middle initial in Joe B. Hall's name stand for?
A. Beasman

Q. Who followed Ed Byhre as coach at Eastern Kentucky in 1981?
A. Max Good

Q. What future politician led UK in assists in 1962?
A. Scotty Baesler (4.3 per game)

Q. Who served as assistant coach to Western Kentucky's Ed Diddle from 1939-64?
A. Ted Hornback

Q. What is the first name of Murray State's "Popeye" Jones?
A. Ronald

Q. What point guard helped lead Murray State to a share of the 1980 OVC championship?
A. Lamont Sleets

Q. Who led UK in scoring during the 1972 and '73 seasons?

A. Jim Andrews (21.5 ppg in '72; 20.1 ppg in '73)

Q. Who led Louisville in free throw shooting three consecutive seasons, 1973-75?
A. Terry Howard

Q. What was the first name of UK All-American "Cotton" Nash?
A. Charles

Q. What moniker was accorded UK's 1971-72 freshmen team?
A. "Super Kittens"

Q. Who followed Guy Strong as Eastern Kentucky coach in 1973?
A. Bob Mulcahy

Q. What Murray State star is credited locally with the invention of the jump shot?
A. Joe Fulks

Q. What future Memphis State coach was a Louisville assistant in Denny Crum's first season as coach of the Cardinals?
A. Dana Kirk

Q. Robert Wilson coached Kentucky Wesleyan from 1943-59. What was his nickname?
A. "Bullet"

Q. Who led UK in scoring in 1950?
A. Bill Spivey (19.3 points per game)

Q. Who was the starting point guard for Louisville's 1980 NCAA champions?
A. Jerry Eaves

Q. What is Paducah Community College's nickname?
A. "Indians"

Q. What future Harlem Globetrotter led Kentucky Wesleyan in scoring and rebounding in 1988?
A. J.B. Brown

Q. Who was a vivacious radio voice of the Western Kentucky Hilltoppers from 1954-81?
A. Bud Tyler

Q. Who led Louisville in scoring three consecutive seasons, 1963-65?
A. John Reuther (16.2 ppg in '63;19.6 ppg in '64; 18.8 ppg in '65)

Q. Who coached Murray State from 1925-41?
A. Carlisle Cutchin

Q. Who led Kentucky in scoring in 1989?
A. LeRon Ellis (16 points per game)

Q. What was the nickname of Kentucky's Kenny Walker?
A. "Sky"

Q. Who led Murray State in scoring in 1966 and '67?
A. Herb McPherson

Q. What were the monikers accorded Adolph Rupp?
A. "The Baron" and "The Man in the Brown Suit"

Q. Who coached Morehead State to a share of the OVC championship in 1969?
A. Bob Wright

Q. Who were the starting forwards on UK's 1946 NIT champions?
A. Jack Tingle and Wilbur Schue

Q. Who led Murray State in rebounding in 1984 and '85?
A. Vada Martin (6.2 rpg in '84; 6.3 rpg in '85)

Q. Who was the first Western Kentucky player to score 1,000 points?
A. Carlisle Towery (1940, 1,010 career points)

Q. In the 1992 book, *Hello Everybody, This is Cawood Ledford,* the UK broadcaster named what two state players to his 10-member UK All-Opponent team, 1953-92?
A. Jim McDaniels (Western Kentucky) and Rodney McCray (Louisville)

Q. Who led Kentucky in free throw shooting in 1969?
A. Phil Argento (77 percent)

Q. What All-SEC performer led UK in rebounding in 1960?
A. Don Mills (12.9 per game)

Q. What future Kentucky Colonels coach and general manager was a Western Kentucky assistant coach from 1964-67?
A. Gene Rhodes

Q. Who was Louisville's first basketball coach?
A. William Gardiner (1911-12, 0-3 record)

Q. What was the nickname of UK guard Adrian Smith?
A. "Odie"

Q. On Jan. 25, 1954, what *Courier-Journal* sportswriter broke the story that UK's Cliff Hagan, Frank Ramsey and Lou Tsioropoulas would be ineligible for that season's NCAA

Tournament because they were fifth-year graduate students?
A. Larry Boeck

Q. What pair of London, Ky. brothers were starters for Louisville's 1948 NAIB champions?
A. Ray "Button" Combs and Glenn "Ish" Combs

Q. What Kentucky Wesleyan All-American was a member of the Harlem Globetrotters from 1970-73?
A. Dallas Thornton

Q. In June, 1990, who became one of the first female assistant coaches of a men's Division I program when she joined Rick Pitino's UK staff?
A. Bernadette Locke-Mattox

Q. What is Kentucky State's nickname?
A. "Thorobreds"

Q. What two monikers were accorded Western Kentucky's Ed Diddle?
A. "Uncle Ed" and "The Man With The Red Towel"

Q. Who is second on the career scoring list at Louisville?
A. Pervis Ellison (2,143 points)

Q. Preseason knee surgery forced what Western Kentucky star to sit out the Hilltoppers' 1971 Final Four season?
A. Jerome Perry

Q. What was the nickname of UK's Richard Madison?
A. "Master Blaster"

Q. Who was the starting point guard for Western Kentucky's 1967 OVC champions?
A. Butch Kaufman

Q. Who coached Kentucky Wesleyan to its fourth NCAA Division II championship in 1973?
A. Bob Jones

Q. What were Louisville's teams of the late-1970s and early-'80s known as?
A. "The Doctors of Dunk"

Q. What was the nickname of UK star Jack Givens?
A. "Goose"

Q. What UK player was a member of the 1977 NBA-champion Portland Trail Blazers?
A. Larry Steele

Q. Who were the starting guards on Adolph Rupp's last UK team, 1971-72?
A. Ronnie Lyons and Stan Key

Q. Who led UK in scoring in 1983?
A. Melvin Turpin (15.1 points per game)

Q. Who followed Jim Richards as coach at Western Kentucky in 1978?
A. Gene Keady

Q. Who were UK's three full-time assistant coaches in Rick Pitino's first season, 1989-90?
A. Ralph Willard, Herb Sendek and Tubby Smith

Q. Who led the Wildcats in scoring when UK defeated Oklahoma A&M 46-36 for the 1949 NCAA title?
A. Alex Groza (25 points)

Q. Who followed Wayne Chapman as Kentucky Wesleyan coach in 1990?
A. Wayne Boultinghouse

Q. What was the nickname of Kentucky State's high-scoring Travis Grant?
A. "The Machine"

Q. Who led Murray State in field goal percentage three consecutive seasons, 1970-72?
A. Bill Mancini

Q. What Morehead State and future Phoenix Suns player led the OVC in rebounding in 1969?
A. Lamar Green (18.1 per game)

Q. In reference to his smooth style of play, what nickname was given to UK's Jack Givens by his teammates?
A. "Silk"

Q. What former Louisville assistant coach was a starting forward at U of L in 1965-66?
A. Wade Houston (10.8 points per game)

Q. What Murray State star was an All-American tennis player in the early-1950s?
A. Bennie Purcell

Q. Who were the starting guards on UK's 1951 NCAA championship team?
A. Frank Ramsey and Bobby Watson

Q. What younger brother of Clem Haskins was a member of UK's 1976 NIT championship team?
A. Merion Haskins

Q. What is Transylvania's nickname?
A. "Pioneers"

Q. What was the nickname of Louisville All-American Charlie Tyra?
A. "The Moose"

Q. What two players led Western Kentucky in scoring when the Hilltoppers defeated Ohio University in the 1960 NCAA Tournament?
A. Don Parson and Charlie Osborne (23 points each)

Q. Through 1990, who were the only three four-year players at Louisville who had not played in the Final Four during the Denny Crum era?
A. Larry Williams (1976-79), Felton Spencer and Craig Hawley (1987-90)

Q. Who transferred from Northern Kentucky and became UK's crowd favorite during the 1992-93 season?
A. Todd Svoboda

Q. Murray State's "Racers" are also known by what other nickname?
A. "Thoroughbreds"

Q. What is the nickname of Sullivan College?
A. "Executives"

Q. What was the name of the first live wildcat given to UK for mascot purposes?
A. "Tom" (died quickly from being in captivity, 1921)

Q. In addition to "Tom," what were the names of the other live wildcat mascots?
A. "TNT," "Whiskers," "Hot Tamale," and "Colonel"

Q. Who made up UK's "Fiddlin' Five" national championship team in 1958?
A. Adrian Smith, Vernon Hatton (guards), Johnny Cox, John Crigler (forward), Ed Beck (center)

Q. Who has been the radio voice of the Kentucky Wesleyan Panthers since 1961?
A. Joel Utley

Q. What was the nickname of Kentucky Wesleyan star Kelly Coleman?
A. "King"

Q. What Western Kentucky All-American teamed with UK All-American Louie Dampier to form the ABA Kentucky Colonels' first backcourt tandem in 1967-68?
A. Darel Carrier

Q. What were Western Kentucky's basketball teams known as before they were known as "Hilltoppers"?
A. "Pedagogues" or "Teachers"

CHAPTER 2

NUMBERS

Q. How many fans greeted the Kentucky basketball team at Lexington's Blue Grass Airport after the Wildcats won the 1978 NCAA championship?
A. 10,000 (estimated)

Q. In Ralph Willard's first three seasons as coach at Western Kentucky (1991-93), what was the Hilltoppers' record in Diddle Arena?
A. 35-6 (.853)

Q. Through 1993, how many Southeastern Conference Tournament championships had UK won?
A. 17 (the last coming in 1993)

Q. When Popeye Jones arrived at Murray State in 1988, what was his reported height and weight?
A. 6-feet-8, 315 pounds

Q. Through 1993, what was Louisville coach Denny Crum's NCAA Tournament won-lost record?
A. 35-17 (fourth on all-time victory list)

Q. How many points did Popeye Jones score in four seasons at Murray State?
A. 2,057 (second in school history)

Q. What does Western Kentucky rank nationally in victories per season?
A. Third (17.35 victories per year in 74 seasons (through '93); North Carolina (18.92) and UCLA (17.49) rank 1-2)

Q. How many times did Murray State win or share the Ohio Valley Conference regular season championship in the 1980s?
A. Five (1980,'82, '83, '88, '89)

Q. What number was worn by Kentucky's Dale Brown?
A. 31

Q. What height was Kentucky's Leroy Byrd?
A. 5-feet-5

Q. What year did UK's Adolph Rupp serve as co-coach of the United States Olympic Basketball Team?
A. 1948

Q. Through 1993, how many consecutive Final Fours had the University of Louisville statistics crew worked?
A. 24

Q. How many state teams reached the "Sweet 16" of the 1993 NCAA Tournament?
A. Three (Kentucky, Louisville, Western Kentucky)

Q. What number was worn by Louisville's Phil Rollins?
A. 9

Q. Through 1993, what was Murray State's record in NCAA Tournament competition?
A. 1-6

Q. How many shots did Louisville guard James Brewer miss in the second half of the Cardinals' victory over Oklahoma State in the 1993 NCAA Tournament?
A. None (He made two three-pointers, two field goals and 10 free throws)

Q. In all sports, what was Ed Diddle's 42-year coaching record at Western Kentucky?
A. 1,043-483-2 (men's basketball, 759-302; women's basketball, 11-6; baseball, 235-151; football 38-24-2)

Q. What number was worn by Murray State's Popeye Jones?
A. 54 (also 34, as freshman)

Q. As a member of Louisville's freshmen team in 1964-65, what were Wes Unseld's scoring and rebounding averages per game?
A. 35.8 points, 23.6 rebounds

Q. How many state teams were ranked in the final Associated Press Top 25 poll of 1993?
A. Three (Kentucky, 2nd; Louisville, 15th; Western Kentucky 20th)

Q. Through 1993, how many Sun Belt Conference Tournament championships had Western Kentucky won?
A. One (1993)

Q. What number was worn by Eastern Kentucky star Bobby Washington?
A. 44

Q. Through 1993, what was UK's record in NCAA Tournament regional championship games?

A. 9-14

Q. How many state teams were ranked in the final regular season CNN/USA Today Top 25 coaches poll of 1993?

A. Three (Kentucky, 3rd; Louisville, 14th; Western Kentucky, 25th)

Q. How many times has Morehead State won 20 games in a season?

A. One (1983-84, 25-6 under Coach Wayne Martin)

Q. What is the jersey number of Louisville star Dwayne Morton?

A. 50

Q. Prior to transferring to Kentucky, in how many NCAA Tournament games had Travis Ford played?

A. One (as a Missouri freshman in 1990, Ford scored three points in the Tigers' 74-71 first-round upset loss to Northern Iowa)

Q. In what season was Louisville's James Brewer redshirted?

A. 1989-90 (following his freshman season of 1988-89)

Q. What number was worn by Western Kentucky point guard Mark Bell?
A. 10

Q. What is the longest streak of improved attendance for Louisville since Freedom Hall opened in 1956?
A. 12 consecutive seasons (1977-78 through 1988-89)

Q. In Rick Pitino's first four seasons as UK coach (1990-93), what was UK's record at Rupp Arena?
A. 57-4 (.934; includes 3-0 record in '93 SEC Tournament)

Q. What number was worn by Murray State star Jim Jennings?
A. 21

Q. How many Kentucky Intercollegiate Athletic Association (KIAC) championships did Ed Diddle's Western Kentucky teams win?
A. 13

Q. What height was UK All-American Cliff Hagan?
A. 6-feet-4

Q. What was Louisville's basketball budget in 1944-45?
A. $3,500

Q. What year did Kentucky become the first team to participate in the NIT and NCAA tournaments in the same season?
A. 1949

Q. What number was worn by Murray State forward Les Taylor?
A. 30

Q. Since joining the Metro Conference in 1975-76, how many regular-season championships has Louisville won?
A. 11 (through 1993)

Q. How many times did Western Kentucky appear in the National Invitation Tournament in the 1950s?
A. Four (1950, '52, '53, '54; won 3, lost 5)

Q. How many home games did Kentucky lose at Rupp Arena during the 1992-93 season?
A. None (13-0)

Q. What number was worn by Louisville center Felton Spencer?
A. 50

Q. How many team and individual NCAA Tournament records did UK's 1949 national champions set?
A. 25

Q. UK's Adolph Rupp coached 19 seasons in Alumni Gym. In 209 home games played there under Rupp, how many times did the Wildcats lose?
A. Eight

Q. What is Western Kentucky's longest winning streak vs. Louisville?
A. 10 games (1938-44)

Q. How many fans welcomed the Louisville basketball team at Standiford Field after the Cardinals' 1956 NIT championship?
A. 5,000 (estimated; police estimated the crowd to be larger than when President Dwight D. Eisenhower visited the city four years earlier)

Q. How many seasons did Bob Davis coach at Georgetown College?
A. 20 (1954-73)

Q. In Centre College's run to the 1979 NCAA Division III Final Four, what was the Colonels' longest winning streak?
A. 18 games (snapped in national semifinals by Potsdam State N.Y., 67-63)

Q. What team leads the all-time series between Kentucky and Louisville?
A. Kentucky (17-7, through 1993)

Q. During the Ed Diddle era at Western Kentucky, what was the Hilltoppers' longest string of yearly appearances at New York's Madison Square Garden?
A. 14 years (1946-47 through 1959-60)

Q. How many times has Kentucky led the nation in home attendance?
A. Eight (in consecutive years, 1977-84)

Q. Darrell Griffith wore what number at Louisville?
A. 35

Q. By what margin does Western Kentucky lead its all-time series with rival Eastern Kentucky?
A. 107-39 (through 1993)

Q. What was Louisville's NCAA Tournament record in the 1980s?
A. 23-6

Q. What was UK's average home game attendance in 1992-93?
A. 24,019 (312,243 for 13 games)

Q. In 23 seasons as Louisville coach, Peck Hickman produced how many 20-victory seasons?
A. 11

Q. What was the height of Louisville forward Bobby Turner?
A. 6-feet-4

Q. In 16 seasons as coach at Murray State, how many losing seasons did Cal Luther record?
A. Two (his first season, 10-15 in 1958-59; and his last season, 12-13 in 1973-74)

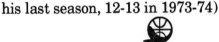

Q. Before arriving at UK in 1989, Rick Pitino had produced how many 20-victory seasons as a collegiate head coach?
A. Two (21-9 in 1979-80, at Boston University; 25-9 in 1986-87, at Providence)

Q. As a UK player, C. M. Newton wore what two uniform numbers?
A. 30 and 35

Q. What was the won-lost record of UK's freshmen team in 1971-72?
A. 22-0

Q. What number was worn by Morehead State scoring sensation Brett Roberts?
A. 30

Q. In 34 seasons as a member of the Ohio Valley Conference, Western Kentucky won how many OVC Tournaments?
A. 10 (34-7 record in tournament play)

Q. What was Kentucky ranked in the final post-season CNN/USA Today coaches Top 25 poll?
A. Third (Louisville was 15th; Western Kentucky was 16th)

Q. For how many NBA teams did Louisville's Phil Rollins play?
A. Four (Philadelphia Warriors, Cincinnati Royals, St. Louis Hawks, New York Knicks)

Q. What was the height of Western Kentucky's Tony Wilson?
A. 6-feet-7

Q. How many fans greeted UK's basketball team at Lexington's Blue Grass Airport after the Wildcats' loss to Duke in the 1992 NCAA Tournament?
A. 5,000 (estimated)

Q. When John Mauer resigned as UK coach in 1930, Adolph Rupp was one of how many candidates for the job?
A. 70

Q. What year did Adolph Rupp record his first 20-victory season at Kentucky?
A. 1932-33 (20-3)

Q. UK opened the 1992-93 season with how many consecutive victories?
A. 11 (streak snapped at Vanderbilt, 101-86, Jan. 13, 1993)

Q. What number was worn by Louisville's Manuel Forrest?
A. 30

Q. How many fans welcomed home UK's 1949 NCAA champions on "Wildcat Appreciate Day," April 4, 1949?
A. 25,000 (estimated)

Q. How many 20-victory seasons were posted by Louisville coach John Dromo?
A. Two (21-7 in 1967-68; 21-6 in 1968-69)

Q. What was the height of UK center Tom Payne?
A. 7-feet-2

Q. Of the 346 UK games played in Memorial Coliseum, how many games did the Wildcats lose?
A. 38

Q. How many victories did Ed Diddle produce in 42 seasons as men's basketball coach at Western Kentucky?
A. 759 (lost 302)

Q. Western Kentucky All-American Bobby Rascoe wore what number?
A. 45

Q. Through 1993, what was Morehead State's record in NCAA Tournament play?
A. 4-6 (five appearances)

Q. In 1980, when Louisville won its first NCAA championship, what were the Cardinals ranked in the final regular season Associated Press poll?
A. Fourth

Q. How many points per game did Dan Issel average as a UK senior in 1969-70?
A. 33.9

Q. What was the height of Western Kentucky's Mark Bell?
A. 5-feet-8

Q. What number did Pat Riley wear at Kentucky?
A. 42

Q. What was the Freedom Hall won-lost record of Louisville's 1980 NCAA title team?
A. 16-0

Q. In five trips to the NCAA Tournament, how many games has Eastern Kentucky won?
A. None (through 1993)

Q. What number did Louie Dampier wear at Kentucky?
A. 10

Q. What was the height of Western Kentucky's Clem Haskins?
A. 6-feet-3

Q. Kentucky won the 1976 NIT. After 20 games that season, what was the Wildcats' record?
A. 10-10

Q. What number was worn by Louisville's Billy Thompson?
A. 55

Q. What was Louisville's record after winning the 1980 NCAA championship?
A. 33-3

Q. What year did Ed Diddle record his first 20-victory season as coach at Western Kentucky?
A. 1933-34 (28-8)

Q. In 23 years as Louisville's coach, Peck Hickman's teams experienced how many losing or .500 seasons?
A. None

Q. What number was worn by UK All-American Alex Groza?
A. 15 (also 36, as a freshman)

Q. How many points did Jim McDaniels score in Western Kentucky's 97-84 victory over Jacksonville at Freedom Hall, Dec. 23, 1970?
A. 46

Q. What number was worn by Louisville legend Wes Unseld?
A. 31

Q. Dan Issel is one of two UK All-Americans to wear the number 44. Who is the other?
A. Cotton Nash (1962-64)

Q. What number was worn by Travis Grant at Kentucky State?
A. 33

Q. What member of UK's "Rupp's Runts" wore number 30?
A. Tommy Kron

Q. How many seasons did Western Kentucky go undefeated in league play as a member of the Ohio Valley Conference?
A. Three (1949-50, 8-0; 1965-66, 14-0; 1969-70, 14-0)

Q. How many 20-victory seasons did Adolph Rupp produce in 41 years at UK?
A. 23

Q. What number was worn by Kentucky's Mike Pratt?
A. 22

Q. In John Oldham's seven years as coach at Western Kentucky, what was the best won-lost record the Hilltoppers produced?
A. 25-3 (.893, 1965-66)

Q. What number was worn by Louisville's Allen Murphy?
A. 20

Q. What was the height of Western Kentucky standout Dwight Smith?
A. 6-feet-5

Q. What number was worn by Kentucky State's Elmore Smith?
A. 25

Q. What was UK's record in Eddie Sutton's final season as Wildcat coach, 1988-89?
A. 13-19

Q. All-OVC guard George Bryant wore what number at Eastern Kentucky?
A. 44

Q. What was Louisville ranked in the final AP and UPI polls of 1967?
A. Second

Q. What number was worn by Kentucky's Kevin Grevey?
A. 35

Q. What was the height of Louisville's Wes Unseld?
A. 6-feet-8

Q. What number was worn by Western Kentucky star Johnny Britt?
A. 20

Q. Through 1993, what was Morehead State's series record against Marshall?
A. 41-43

Q. What number was worn by Kentucky's Bob Guyette?
A. 45

Q. Adolph Rupp-coached Kentucky teams won or shared how many SEC championships?
A. 27

Q. What was UK's 1992-93 record?
A. 30-4

Q. In Western Kentucky's first visit to Rupp Arena, UK defeated the Hilltoppers by what score?
A. 93-83 (Feb. 15, 1992)

Q. What number was worn by Louisville "super sub" Poncho Wright?
A. 44

Q. What was Jamal Mashburn's final ranking on the all-time UK scoring list?
A. Fourth (1,843 points)

Q. What was the height of UK's Alex Groza?
A. 6-feet-7

Q. By how many victories did UK trail North Carolina on the all-time NCAA victory list entering the 1993-94 season?
A. 10 (North Carolina has won 1,560, UK 1,660)

Q. Of UK's top 10 Rupp Arena crowds, how many have been during the Rick Pitino era?
A. Nine

Q. How many consecutive games had Temple won before losing to Kentucky 61-60 in the 1958 Final Four semifinals?
A. 25

Q. What was UK's record in Adolph Rupp's final season as coach, 1971-72?
A. 21-7 (14-4 in SEC)

Q. What year did Rick Pitino graduate from the University of Massachusetts?
A. 1974

Q. What number was worn by Kentucky's Kyle Macy?
A. 4

Q. What was the height of Western Kentucky All-American Jim McDaniels?
A. 7 feet (upon arrival to the American Basketball Association, McDaniels was measured at 6-feet-10)

Q. What member of UK's "Rupp's Runts" wore number 40?
A. Larry Conley

Q. How many times was UK legend Cawood Ledford named Kentucky Sportscaster of the Year?
A. 22

Q. By what margin did Kentucky defeat Louisville in the 1948 Olympic Trials?
A. 91-57 (at New York)

Q. What number was worn by Western Kentucky star Greg Smith?
A. 34

Q. What number was worn by Louisville's Robbie Valentine?
A. 00

Q. How many seasons did John Dromo serve as an assistant coach under Louisville's Peck Hickman?
A. 19

Q. What was UK ranked in the final AP poll of 1991?
A. Ninth

Q. What number was worn by Louisville's Wiley Brown?
A. 41

Q. What was Kyle Macy's three-year free throw percentage at Kentucky?
A. .890 (331 of 372)

Q. How many points did Jim McDaniels score in Western Kentucky's 1971 NCAA Tournament victory over Kentucky?
A. 35

Q. What was the height of UK guard Louie Damper?
A. 6 feet

Q. What was Kentucky ranked in the final AP poll of 1958?
A. Fifth

Q. How many times did UK produce first-team AP All-Americas in the 1950s?
A. Four (Bill Spivey, 1950; Cliff Hagan, 1952 and '54; Johnny Cox, 1959)

Q. In Louisville's NAIB championship season of 1947-48, how many times were the Cardinals defeated by Western Kentucky?
A. Three (71-44, 77-55, 63-62)

Q. How many consecutive games had Kentucky won entering the 1993 Final Four?
A. 10

Q. What number was worn by UK's Dwane Casey?
A. 20

Q. What is the UK record for consecutive season-opening victories?
A. 37 (1927-61)

Q. What number was worn by Kentucky favorite Richie Farmer?
A. 32

Q. What UK playerss ranked 1-2 in career scoring in the American Basketball Association?
A. 1. Louie Damper (13,725 points); 2. Dan Issel (12,823)

Q. What number was worn by Louisville's Scooter McCray?
A. 21

Q. In 13 seasons at Kentucky, how many games did Coach Joe B. Hall win?
A. 297 (lost 100)

Q. Denny Crum has been coach or assistant coach on how many NCAA championship teams?
A. Seven (coach of Louisville, 1980 and '86; assistant to John Wooden at UCLA, 1967, '68, '69, '70, '71)

Q. From 1980-90, how many Louisville games were network-televised?
A. 69

Q. In seven seasons at his alma mater, Murray State, how many 20-victory seasons were produced by Coach Ron Greene?
A. Three (1980, 23-8; 1982, 20-8; 1983, 21-8)

Q. What is Louisville's longest winning streak?
A. 18 games (1979-80; snapped by Iona 77-60 at Madison Square Garden - the Cardinals' final loss of the season)

Q. What number was worn by UK All-American Jamal Mashburn?
A. 24

Q. What was the height of UK guard Jay Shidler?
A. 6-feet-1

Q. What was Western Kentucky's ranking in the final AP poll of 1950?
A. Eighth

Q. What was the height of Kentucky's Cotton Nash?
A. 6-feet-5

Q. What number was worn by UK All-American Frank Ramsey?
A. 30

Q. How many 20-victory seasons were produced by Western Kentucky's Ed Diddle?
A. 18

Q. How many UK players were double-digit scorers during the Wildcats' NCAA championship season of 1977-78?
A. Five (Jack Givens, 18.1 points per game; Rick Robey, 14.4; Kyle Macy 12.5; James Lee, 11.3; Mike Phillips, 10.2)

Q. What was Louisville's record during Wes Unseld's three varsity seasons, 1966-68?
A. 60-22

Q. By what score did Kentucky defeat Western Kentucky in the second round of the 1986 NCAA Tournament?
A. 71-64 (at Charlotte, N.C.; Clem Haskins' last game as WKU coach)

Q. What number did UK star Cliff Hagan don at Kentucky?
A. 6

Q. In UK's 1978 NCAA championship season, what was the Wildcats' Rupp Arena record?
A. 16-0

Q. How many 20-victory seasons did Murray State produce in the 1960s?
A. One (22-6 in 1968-69)

Q. What number was worn by Louisville star Charlie Tyra?
A. 8

Q. UK holds the record for producing how many consecutive Southeastern Conference victories?
A. 51 (Jan 28, 1950 to Jan. 8, 1955)

Q. How many times did Clem Haskins win the OVC's Player of the Year award?
A. Three (1965-67)

Q. By what score did eventual national champion Kansas defeat Murray State in the second round of the 1988 NCAA Tournament?
A. 61-58 (at Lincoln, Neb.)

Q. What was the height of UK All-American Ralph Beard?
A. 5-feet-10

Q. How many teams were ranked ahead of Kentucky in the final AP poll of 1955?
A. One (eventual NCAA champion San Francisco)

Q. What number did both Dee Gibson and Jim Rose wear at Western Kentucky?
A. 11

Q. In 23 seasons as Louisville coach, how many games did Peck Hickman win?
A. 443 (lost 183)

Q. What number was worn by Louisville star Butch Beard?
A. 14

Q. What was C. M. Newton's 12-year coaching record at Transylvania?
A. 169-137

Q. What number was worn by Western Kentucky All-American Odie Spears?
A. 39

Q. By what score did Louisville defeat Kentucky in the "Dream Game" of the 1983 NCAA Tournament?
A. 80-68 in overtime (at Knoxville, Tenn.)

Q. What number was worn by UK guard Truman Claytor?
A. 22

Q. How many points per game did Jim McDaniels average as a junior at Western Kentucky, 1969-70?
A. 28.6

Q. In a series that dates back to 1926, what is Louisville's largest margin of victory over Western Kentucky?
A. 26 points (107-81, at Freedom Hall, Dec. 26, 1974)

Q. What number was worn by Louisville's Everick Sullivan?
A. 34

Q. How many games has Louisville played in Broadbent Arena?
A. One (U of L defeated Alcorn State 77-75 in a first-round NIT game, Mar. 14, 1985)

Q. What number was worn by Western Kentucky's Chuck Rawlings?
A. 15

Q. During the 1989-90 season Kansas defeated Kentucky by what score?
A. 150-95 (Dec. 9, 1989, at Lawrence, Kan.)

Q. What is Eastern Kentucky's largest margin of victory over rival Western Kentucky in a series that began in 1915?
A. 30 points (99-69, Jan. 13, 1968, at Richmond)

Q. What was Kentucky's record against Notre Dame in games played in the 1960s?
A. 10-1

Q. What was UK ranked in the final AP poll of 1968?
A. Fifth

Q. What was Louisville's record in games played at the Jefferson County Armory?
A. 153-23 (.869)

Q. What is Western Kentucky's largest margin of victory in Diddle Arena?
A. 66 points (123-57 over Tampa, Dec. 10, 1966)

Q. What number was worn by Morehead State star Herbie Stamper?
A. 32

Q. How many points did UK's Jack Givens score in the 1978 NCAA Tournament championship game against Duke?
A. 41

Q. What year did UK capture its first NCAA championship?
A. 1948 (36-3 record)

Q. What number did Ralph Beard wear at Kentucky?
A. 12 (also 38)

Q. By what score did Texas Western defeat Kentucky in the 1966 NCAA Tournament championship game?
A. 72-65 (at College Park, Md.)

Q. What number was worn by Western Kentucky All-American John Oldham?
A. 42

CHAPTER 3

GAMES

Q. What team did Kentucky defeat in the third round of the 1993 NCAA Tournament?
A. Wake Forest (103-69, at Charlotte, N.C.)

Q. What added significance to Louisville's 98-75 victory over South Florida, Jan. 7, 1993, at Freedom Hall?
A. It was Denny Crum's 500th victory as Cardinal coach.

Q. What team did Western Kentucky defeat in the first round of the 1993 NCAA Tournament?
A. Memphis State (55-52, at Orlando, Fla.)

Q. Who led Kentucky in scoring and rebounding in the Wildcats' loss to Duke in the 1992 NCAA Tournament?
A. Jamal Mashburn (28 points, 10 rebounds)

Q. By what score did UK defeat rival Tennessee in the first round of the 1993 SEC Tournament?
A. 101-40 (at Rupp Arena)

Q. Who made a top-of-the-key jump shot to give Western Kentucky a 94-93 overtime victory over Eastern Kentucky in 1971, clinching the Ohio Valley Conference title for the Hilltoppers?
A. Danny Johnson (game played at Richmond)

Q. What team did Kentucky defeat to win the championship game of the 1950 SEC Tournament?
A. Tennessee (91-58, at Louisville)

Q. What team did Louisville defeat to win the championship game of the 1957 Bluegrass Invitational Tournament?
A. Dayton (61-53 in overtime, at Louisville)

Q. What team did UK defeat to win the championship game of the 1992 SEC Tournament?
A. Alabama (80-54, at Birmingham, Ala.)

Q. Besides Jack Givens, who was UK's only double-digit scorer in the Wildcats' NCAA title game victory over Duke in 1978?
A. Rick Robey (20 points)

Q. What team defeated Murray State in the first round of the 1992 NCAA Tournament?
A. Arkansas (80-69, at Milwaukee, Wisc.)

Q. What was UK's second-half field goal percentage in the Wildcats' 53-40 loss to Georgetown in the 1984 Final Four semifinals?
A. Nine percent (3 of 33; game played at Seattle's Kingdome)

Q. What team defeated Western Kentucky in the third round of the 1993 NCAA Tournament?
A. Florida State (81-78 in overtime, at Charlotte, N.C.)

Q. What team upset Kentucky in the second round of the Preseason NIT in 1991?
A. Pittsburgh (85-67, at Rupp Arena)

Q. What team did Western Kentucky defeat in the 1993 Sun Belt Conference Tournament championship game?
A. New Orleans (72-63; UNO ranked No. 13 and winner of 20 consecutive league games)

Q. By what margin did Michigan defeat Kentucky in the 1993 Final Four semifinals?
A. 81-78 in overtime (at Louisiana Superdome, New Orleans)

Q. The NCAA imposed a one season ban on UK (1989-90) from appearing on live television as part of the program's probation. Who did the Wildcats play in their first live TV game of 1990-91?

A. Cincinnati (UK won 75-71 on ESPN, Dec. 28, 1990, at Cincinnati)

Q. On Feb. 16, 1960, what caused Eastern Kentucky coach Paul McBrayer to remove his team from the floor in a game at Western Kentucky?

A. McBrayer felt that Western coach Ed Diddle tried to "attack" Eastern's Ralph Richardson, who collided with Western's Bobby Rascoe and hurdled into the Western bench (Western led 38-20 at the time of the forfeit).

Q. In the 1975 Final Four semifinals, what was the score of the Louisville-UCLA game at the end of regulation?

A. 65-65 (UCLA won in overtime on a basket by Richard Washington, 75-74)

Q. Who missed a free throw with one second to play, allowing Ohio State to escape with a 56-55 victory over Louisville in the 1961 NCAA Mideast Regional Tournament at Freedom Hall?

A. All-American John Turner

Q. What team did Louisville defeat in the second round of the 1993 NCAA Tournament?

A. Oklahoma State (78-63, at Indianapolis)

Q. Who hit a 47-foot shot at the buzzer to send the Dec. 7, 1957 UK-Temple game into the second of three overtimes?
A. Vernon Hatton (who scored six of UK's eight points in the third OT; UK won, 85-83)

Q. What team did Murray State defeat to win the 1992 OVC Tournament championship game?
A. Eastern Kentucky (81-60, at Rupp Arena)

Q. What was the sociologically significant aspect of the UK-Texas Western NCAA championship game of 1966?
A. It marked the first time a team with an all-white starting lineup (Kentucky) played a team with an all-black starting lineup (Texas Western) for the NCAA title (event is often referred to as "Basketball's Brown vs. Board of Education Game").

Q. Who scored a basket in the closing seconds to give Western Kentucky a 74-72 victory over West Virginia in the first round of the 1987 NCAA Tournament?
A. Kannard Johnson

Q. What team did Louisville defeat for its only victory of the 1939-40 season?
A. Berea (56-55 in the first round of the KIAC Tournament, at Richmond; U of L finished the season 1-18)

Q. Who heaved an inbounds pass three-quarters of the court to set up Christian Laettner's game-winning basket when Duke defeated UK 104-103 in the finals of the 1992 NCAA East Regional Tournament?
A. Grant Hill

Q. What team did Georgetown College upset in the NAIA national quarterfinals in 1993?
A. David Lipscomb (101-91, at Kansas City, Mo.)

Q. What team did Kentucky defeat in the first round of the 1993 NCAA Tournament?
A. Rider (96-52, at Nashville, Tenn.)

Q. What ailment hampered UK's Cliff Hagan in the Wildcats' 1951 NCAA Tournament championship game victory over Kansas State?
A. Throat infection

Q. In Kentucky's 1958 NCAA Tournament title game victory over Seattle, who led the Wildcats in scoring?
A. Vernon Hatton (30 points)

Q. What team defeated Western Kentucky in the first round of the 1970 NCAA Tournament?
A. Jacksonville (109-96, at Dayton, Ohio)

Q. What team eliminated Louisville in the third round of the 1993 NCAA Tournament?

A. Top-ranked Indiana (82-69, at St. Louis, Mo.)

Q. How many points did Kentucky State's Travis Grant score in the Thorobreds' 102-82 victory over Eastern Michigan for the 1971 NAIA championship?
A. 43

Q. In Western Kentucky's 81-78 victory over Ohio State in the 1971 NCAA Tournament, what Hilltopper hit a baseline jumper to send the game into overtime?
A. Rex Bailey

Q. When Kentucky and Western Kentucky met for the first time in the 1971 NCAA Tournament, did UK wear white or blue uniforms?
A. White (UK was designated the home team; WKU wore road red)

Q. What team did UK defeat in Joe B. Hall's first game as Wildcat coach, Dec. 2, 1972?
A. Michigan State (75-66, at East Lansing, Mich.)

Q. What team did Morehead State defeat in the first round of the first OVC Tournament in 1949?
A. Evansville (57-54, at Louisville)

Q. What team did Western Kentucky upset in the second round of the 1993 NCAA Tournament?
A. Sixth-ranked Seton Hall (72-68, at Orlando, Fla.)

Q. What UK player hit an off-balance bank shot to give the Wildcats a 103-102 lead over Duke with 2.1 seconds remaining in the finals of the 1992 NCAA East Regional Tournament?
A. Sean Woods

Q. The University of Kentucky Invitational Tournament was discontinued following the '89-90 season. What team defeated the Wildcats in the championship game of the final UKIT?
A. Southwestern Louisiana (116-113 in overtime, Dec. 23, 1989)

Q. What team did UK defeat in the finals of the 1993 NCAA Southeast Regional Tournament, earning a trip to the Final Four?
A. Florida State (106-91, at Charlotte, N.C.)

Q. What year did UK's Gimel Martinez and Travis Ford face each other as high school players?
A. 1987 (Martinez' Miami Fla. Senior team defeated Ford's Madisonville-North Hopkins team 76-70 in the championship game of the Kissimee Fla. Shootout)

Q. What two teams did Western Kentucky defeat to win the 1967 All-Sports Classic at Dallas?
A. Indiana (110-91) and California (96-85)

Q. Who hit a three-point shot from the corner to give Western Kentucky a 78-77 victory over Louisville at Freedom Hall, Feb. 16, 1993?
A. Darrin Horn (Western's first victory over U of L since March 1, 1961)

Q. What team did UK defeat in the second round of the 1993 NCAA Tournament?
A. Utah (83-62, at Nashville, Tenn.)

Q. What team eliminated Georgetown College in the NAIA national semifinals in 1993?
A. Oklahoma Baptist (83-69, at Kansas City, Mo.)

Q. Where was the 1992 Kentucky-Duke NCAA East Regional championship game played?
A. The Spectrum (Philadelphia)

Q. What team did Louisville defeat to win the 1986 Metro Conference Tournament?
A. Memphis State (88-79, at Freedom Hall)

Q. In Louisville's first basketball game, what team defeated the Cardinals?
A. Louisville YMCA (35-3, Jan. 28, 1912)

Q. What team did Kentucky State defeat to win its third consecutive NAIA national championship in 1972?
A. Eau Claire, Wisc. (71-62, at Kansas City, Mo.)

Q. What team did UK defeat in the Wildcats' first game in Memorial Coliseum?
A. West Texas State (73-43, Dec. 1, 1950)

Q. What team defeated Morehead State in Ellis Johnson's final game as Eagles coach?
A. Western Kentucky (76-65, in second round of the 1953 OVC Tournament, at Louisville)

Q. Who hit a "Hail Mary" shot behind midcourt at the buzzer to give Arkansas a 74-73 victory over Louisville in the second round of the 1981 NCAA Tournament?
A. U. S. Reed (at Austin, Tex.)

Q. What team did Eastern Kentucky defeat to win the 1950 OVC Tournament championship game?
A. Western Kentucky (62-50, at Louisville)

Q. What team did Kentucky Wesleyan defeat to win the 1990 NCAA Division II Tournament championship game?
A. Gannon (92-74, at Springfield, Mass.)

Q. What team defeated Murray State in the first round of the 1982 NIT?
A. UNLV (87-61, at Las Vegas, Nev.)

Q. What team defeated Louisville in the consolation game of the 1985 NIT?
A. Tennessee (100-84, at Madison Square Garden)

Q. What team did Kentucky defeat in the third round of the 1984 NCAA Tournament?
A. Louisville (72-67, at Rupp Arena)

Q. What team did UK defeat to win the 1986 SEC Tournament title?
A. Alabama (83-72, at Rupp Arena)

Q. What team did Louisville defeat in a Missouri Valley Conference playoff game in 1972?
A. Memphis State (83-72, at Nashville, Tenn.)

Q. In 1993, the NCAA recognized a 1932 UK basketball victory that pushed Adolph Rupp's victory total to 876. What team did the Wildcats defeat?
A. A group of UK basketball alumni

Q. What team did Kentucky defeat for its first NCAA Tournament victory?
A. Illinois (46-44, 1942)

Q. What team did Louisville defeat to win the 1986 NCAA Tournament championship game?
A. Duke (72-69, at Dallas)

Q. What team did Murray State defeat in Cal Luther's first game as Racers coach?
A. Texas Wesleyan (70-56, Dec. 1, 1958, at Racer Arena)

Q. In 1989 Rick Pitino recorded his first victory as UK coach against what team?
A. Ohio University (76-73, at Rupp Arena)

Q. What team did Louisville defeat in the first round of the 1993 NCAA Tournament?
A. Delaware (76-70, at Indianapolis)

Q. What team did Kentucky defeat to win the 1949 NCAA championship?
A. Oklahoma A&M (46-36, at Seattle)

Q. What team did Louisville defeat to win its first NCAA championship in 1980?
A. UCLA (59-54, at Indianapolis)

Q. What team did Louisville defeat in the championship game of the 1982 Great Alaska Shootout?
A. Vanderbilt (80-70)

Q. What team eliminated Morehead State from the 1961 NCAA Tournament?
A. Kentucky (71-64, at Freedom Hall)

Q. What team did Murray State upset in the first round of the 1988 NCAA Tournament?
A. North Carolina State (78-75, at Lincoln, Neb.)

Q. What team defeated Western Kentucky in the "Dedication Game" for E. A. Diddle Arena, Dec. 1, 1963?
A. Vanderbilt (82-60)

Q. What streak did Louisville bring to an end on Valentine's Day, 1993?
A. UNLV's nation-leading streak of 59 consecutive home victories (U of L won 90-86 at the Thomas & Mack Center)

Q. What team did UK defeat in the Wildcats' first televised game?
A. St. John's (59-43, Mar. 22, 1951, at New York)

Q. What team did UK defeat in the 1966 Final Four semifinals?
A. Duke (83-79, at College Park, Md.)

Q. What team upset Kentucky in the first round of the 1949 NIT?
A. Loyola of Chicago (67-56)

Q. What team eliminated Western Kentucky from the 1978 NCAA Tournament?
A. Michigan State (90-69, at Dayton, Ohio)

Q. What team did Louisville defeat to win the 1971 ECAC Holiday Festival at New York's Madison Square Garden?
A. Fordham (96-82)

Q. What team defeated Western Kentucky in the championship game of the 1986 Preseason NIT?
A. UNLV (96-95 in overtime, at Madison Square Garden)

Q. What team eliminated Louisville from the 1977 NCAA Tournament?
A. UCLA (87-79, at Pocatello, Id.)

Q. What team eliminated Louisville in the first round of the 1952 NIT?
A. Western Kentucky (62-59)

Q. Adolph Rupp's last victory as UK coach came against what team in the 1972 NCAA Tournament?
A. Marquette (85-69, at Dayton, Ohio)

Q. What team eliminated Morehead State from the 1983 NCAA Tournament?
A. Syracuse (74-59, at Hartford, Conn.)

Q. What team defeated Louisville in both the 1983 and '84 editions of the Chaminade Classic?
A. Chaminade (89-71 in '83; 67-65 in '84)

Q. What team defeated Murray State in the first round of the 1983 NIT?
A. Wake Forest (87-80, at Racer Arena)

Q. What team did UK defeat in the first round of the 1951 NCAA Tournament?
A. Louisville (79-68, at Raleigh, N.C.)

Q. Western Kentucky upset what team in the first round of the 1978 NCAA Tournament?
A. Syracuse (87-86 in overtime, at Knoxville, Tenn.; many believe this victory saved the OVC's automatic berth in the NCAA Tournament)

Q. What team defeated Western Kentucky in the championship game of the 1942 NIT?
A. West Virginia (47-45)

Q. What team handed UK its only regular season loss of the 1965-66 season?
A. Tennessee (69-62, at Knoxville, Tenn.)

Q. What team eliminated Murray State in the first round of the 1964 NCAA Tournament?
A. Loyola of Chicago (101-91, at Evanston, Ill.)

Q. What team did Kentucky defeat in the third round of the 1958 NCAA Tournament?
A. Notre Dame (89-56, at Lexington)

Q. What team defeated Murray State in the first round of the 1969 NCAA Tournament?
A. Marquette (82-62, at Carbondale, Ill.)

Q. Before running off 21 consecutive victories, Western Kentucky lost to what team in its 1966-67 opener?
A. Vanderbilt (76-70, at Diddle Arena)

Q. What team did UK defeat to win the Sugar Bowl Tournament, Dec. 29, 1956?
A. Houston (111-76, at New Orleans)

Q. What team upset Kentucky in the first round of the UKIT, Dec. 22, 1978?
A. Texas A&M (73-69)

Q. What team eliminated UK from the 1973 NCAA Tournament?
A. Indiana (72-65, at Nashville, Tenn.)

Q. What team did Kentucky defeat to win the 1948 NCAA Tournament championship game?
A. Baylor (58-42, at New York)

Q. What team stunned No. 1 Kentucky in the finals of the 1951 SEC Tournament?
A. Vanderbilt (61-57, at Louisville)

Q. What team did Kentucky defeat 106-100 in overtime in the 1973 NCAA Tournament?
A. Austin Peay (at Nashville, Tenn.)

Q. What team did Murray State upset in the second round of the 1980 NIT?
A. Alabama (70-62, at Tuscaloosa, Ala.)

Q. What team defeated Louisville in the consolation game of the 1972 Final Four?
A. North Carolina (105-91, at Los Angeles)

Q. What team defeated Louisville in the first round of the 1984 Wendy's Classic?
A. Louisiana Tech (73-64, at Bowling Green)

Q. What team stunned Western Kentucky in John Oldham's first game as Hilltopper coach, Dec. 1, 1964?
A. Belmont (Tenn.) College (52-50, at Diddle Arena)

Q. What team defeated Murray State in the 1952 NAIA championship game?
A. Southwest Missouri (73-64)

Q. What team did Western Kentucky defeat in the first round of the 1966 NCAA Tournament?
A. Loyola of Chicago (105-84, at Kent, Ohio)

Q. What team did UK defeat in the Wildcats' first televised SEC game?
A. Louisiana State (76-61, Jan. 10, 1959, at Baton Rouge, La.)

Q. Who won the first game played between Kentucky and Louisville?
A. Kentucky (34-10, Feb. 15, 1913, at Lexington)

Q. What team defeated Western Kentucky at Freedom Hall during the 1971-72 season?
A. Pennsylvania (88-79, Dec. 23, 1971)

Q. What team defeated Eastern Kentucky in the first round of the 1972 NCAA Tournament?
A. Florida State (83-81, at Knoxville, Tenn.)

Q. What two teams played in the "Dedication Game" for Freedom Hall, Dec. 19, 1956?
A. Western Kentucky and defending NCAA champion San Francisco (Western won, 61-57)

Q. What team did Morehead State defeat in the first round of the 1961 NCAA Tournament?
A. Xavier of Ohio (71-66, at Freedom Hall)

Q. Western Kentucky recorded its 1,000th basketball victory against what team?
A. Murray State (82-81, Feb. 19, 1977, at Racer Arena)

Q. What team defeated Louisville in Peck Hickman's last game as Cardinal coach?
A. Kansas (70-68, in the consolation game of the 1967 NCAA Midwest Regional)

Q. What team defeated Louisville in the first round of the 1983 Chaminade Classic?
A. Houston (76-73)

Q. What team did Louisville defeat in the championship game of the 1966 Quaker City Classic?
A. Princeton (72-63, at Philadelphia)

Q. What team did UK defeat in the finals of the 1953-54 UKIT?
A. Eventual NCAA champion LaSalle (73-60)

Q. What team defeated Louisville in three overtimes in the first round of the 1966 NIT?
A. Boston College (96-90)

Q. What team did UK defeat in the championship game of the first SEC Tournament in 1933?
A. Mississippi (46-27, at Atlanta, Ga.)

Q. Where did Western Kentucky defeat Evansville 75-63, Jan. 10, 1951?
A. Owensboro Sportscenter

Q. What team did Louisville defeat to win the championship game of the 1978 Metro Conference Tournament?
A. Florida State (94-93, at Cincinnati, Ohio)

Q. What team eliminated Louisville in the second round of the 1990 NCAA Tournament?
A. Ball State (62-60, at Salt Lake City, Utah)

Q. As a player at Holy Cross, what year did Western Kentucky coach Ralph Willard face the Hilltoppers?
A. 1967 (WKU defeated the Crusaders 90-84 in the first round of the Hurricane Classic, Dec. 27, at Miami Beach, Fla.)

Q. What team upset Kentucky in the 1955 NCAA Tournament?
A. Marquette (79-71, at Evanston, Ill.)

Q. What team did Louisville defeat in the 1980 Final Four semifinals?
A. Iowa (80-71, at Indianapolis)

Q. What team defeated Western Kentucky in the first round of the 1967 NCAA Tournament?
A. Dayton (69-67 in overtime, at Lexington)

Q. What team did Kentucky defeat in the finals of the 1958 UKIT?
A. West Virginia (97-91)

Q. What team handed UK its only regular season loss of 1950-51 in the first round of the Sugar Bowl Tournament?
A. St. Louis (43-42, at New Orleans)

Q. What team did Western Kentucky defeat in the first round of the 1986 Preseason NIT?
A. Notre Dame (80-63, at South Bend, Ind.)

Q. What team pulled off a stunning upset against Kentucky in the 1982 NCAA Tournament?
A. Middle Tennessee (50-44, at Nashville, Tenn.)

Q. What team did Louisville defeat to win its Holiday Classic in 1976?
A. Creighton (69-66 in two overtimes)

Q. What team defeated Louisville in the semifinals of the 1959 Final Four?
A. West Virginia (94-79, at Louisville)

Q. Who won the first game played between Western Kentucky and Eastern Kentucky?
A. Western Kentucky (26-21, in 1915, at Bowling Green)

Q. What team defeated Kentucky Wesleyan in the first round of the 1985 Wendy's Classic?
A. Auburn (80-71, at Diddle Arena)

Q. What team defeated Georgetown College in the 1961 NAIA championship game?
A. Grambling State (95-72)

Q. In Louisville's 1983 NCAA Tournament victory over Kentucky, who led the Cardinals in scoring?
A. Lancaster Gordon (24 points)

CHAPTER 4

HONORS

Q. What UK star was named Most Outstanding Player of the 1993 NCAA Southeast Regional Tournament?
A. Travis Ford

Q. What Morehead State standout was the Ohio Valley Conference Player of the Year in 1992?
A. Brett Roberts

Q. What players have had their jersey numbers retired by Murray State University?
A. Popeye Jones (54), Jeff Martin (15), Garrett Beshear (16), Howie Crittenden (19), Bennie Purcell (21), Paul King (30)

Q. What publication named UK coach Rick Pitino national Coach of the Year in 1991?
A. *The Sporting News*

Q. What Western Kentucky player was selected to participate in the National Association of Basketball Coaches All-Star Game at the conclusion of the 1992-93 season?
A. Darnell Mee (West squad)

Q. What Kentucky star was named Most Valuable Player of the 1992 SEC Tournament?
A. Jamal Mashburn

Q. What Louisville standout was named Metro Conference Player of the Year in 1993?
A. Clifford Rozier

Q. How many times did UK's Adolph Rupp win national Coach of the Year recognition?
A. Four

Q. In 1986, what Louisville player became the first freshman since 1944 to be named the NCAA Tournament's Most Outstanding Player?
A. Pervis Ellison

Q. Kentucky's Jamal Mashburn shared the 1993 Associated Press SEC Player of the Year honor with what player?
A. Billy McCaffrey (Vanderbilt)

Q. The jerseys of what three former UK stars were retired by the university in 1992?
A. Louie Dampier, Jack Givens, Carey Spicer

Q. What former Murray State star was selected to the National Basketball Association's Silver Anniversary Team in 1971?
A. Joe Fulks

Q. What Western Kentucky star was named Most Valuable Player of the 1993 Portsmouth Invitational All-Star Tournament, featuring some of the nation's top seniors?
A. Mark Bell

Q. What statewide honor was accorded UK broadcaster Cawood Ledford by the *Lexington Herald-Leader* in 1991?
A. Sportsman of the Year

Q. What Western Kentucky star was named Most Valuable Player of the 1993 Sun Belt Conference Tournament?
A. Darnell Mee

Q. Who was Eastern Kentucky's only All-Ohio Valley Conference selection in both 1974 and '76?
A. Carl Brown

Q. Who was Western Kentucky's only All-OVC selection in 1972?
A. Jerry Dunn

Q. What former Sullivan College and Western Kentucky star was selected as Holland's top professional basketball player for the 1992-93 season?
A. Jack Jennings

Q. What two Murray State players were All-OVC selections in 1992?
A. Popeye Jones and Frank Allen

Q. Who was UK's only All-SEC first-team selection in both 1992 and '93?
A. Jamal Mashburn

Q. What Kentucky player was named MVP of the 1936 SEC Tournament?
A. Whitey Anderson

Q. Who was an All-OVC selection for Murray State from 1951-53?
A. Garrett Beshear

Q. What year was UK coach Adolph Rupp elected to the University of Kansas Hall of Fame?
A. 1959

Q. What two UK players earned All-SEC Tournament honors four consecutive years, 1946-49?
A. Ralph Beard and Wallace Jones

Q. What UK player was the inaugural winner of the Reggie Hanson Sacrifice Award in 1991?
A. Deron Feldhaus

Q. Who was Morehead State's first All-American?
A. Earl Cooper (1943)

Q. What two players shared UK's 110 Percenter award in 1979?
A. Dwight Anderson and Lavon Williams

Q. What UK player was an Associated Press second-team All-SEC selection in 1993?
A. Travis Ford

Q. *Basketball Weekly* selected what Louisville player as an All-American in 1978?
A. Rick Wilson

Q. What Kentucky player was an All-American selection in 1939?
A. Bernard Opper

Q. What two Louisville players shared the team's Most Valuable Player award in 1993?
A. Dwayne Morton and Clifford Rozier

Q. Who was Louisville's first All-American?
A. Charlie Tyra (1956)

Q. The jersey numbers of what four Louisville players are retired by the university?
A. Pervis Ellison (42), Darrell Griffith (35), Wes Unseld (31), Charlie Tyra (8)

Q. What trio of UK players were named to the NCAA Southeast Regional all-tournament team in 1993?
A. Travis Ford, Jamal Mashburn, Jared Prickett

Q. What trio of Kentucky players were All-Southern Conference selections in 1931?
A. George Yates, Louis McGinnis, Carey Spicer

Q. In what regular season tournament was Western Kentucky's Jim McDaniels named Most Valuable Player, 1970-71?
A. ECAC Holiday Festival (at Madison Square Garden)

Q. Who was the only UK player named to the five-player Final Four all-tournament team in 1975?
A. Kevin Grevey

Q. What seven basketball coaches and players were charter members of the Western Kentucky University Athletic Hall of Hall of Fame in '91?
A. Ed Diddle (coach); Dee Gibson, Clem Haskins, Jim McDaniels, John Oldham, Max Reed, Bobby Rascoe (players)

Q. What Louisville star was named Most Outstanding Player of the 1990 Metro Conference Tournament?
A. Felton Spencer

Q. What native of Knoxville, Tenn. was named UK's Student-Athlete of the Year in 1981?
A. Chris Gettelfinger

Q. Who was Morehead State's only All-OVC selection in 1975?
A. Arch Johnson

Q. Who was voted Kentucky's Best Defensive Player in the Wildcats' NCAA runner-up season of 1975?
A. Mike Flynn

Q. What Western Kentucky star was a second-team Associated Press, United Press International, and *Look* magazine All-American as a senior in 1954?
A. Tom Marshall

Q. What Bellarmine star was Great Lakes Valley Conference Player of the Year in 1984?
A. Buddy Cox

Q. Who won UK's Student-Athlete of the Year award in 1992?
A. Travis Ford

Q. What publication named Rick Pitino national Coach of the Year in his second season as Wildcat coach, 1991?
A. *Basketball Times*

Q. What Louisville star was the first Metro Conference Freshman of the Year in 1977?
A. Darrell Griffith

Q. What Louisville standout was a Helms Foundation All-American in 1961?
A. John Turner

Q. What Western Kentucky player was named to the 1993 NCAA Southeast Regional all-tournament team?
A. Mark Bell

Q. What Louisville guard was an All-Metro Conference selection in 1985 and '86?
A. Milt Wagner

Q. What year did Louisville's Denny Crum win his only Missouri Valley Conference Coach of the Year award?
A. 1973

Q. What UK player was named MVP of the 1966 NCAA Mideast Regional Tournament?
A. Pat Riley

Q. What two UK players earned Academic All-SEC honors in 1988?
A. Rex Chapman and Cedric Jenkins

Q. What award did Denny Crum receive from *Basketball Weekly* in 1986?
A. Man of the Year

Q. How many times was Kentucky Wesleyan's Wayne Chapman named NCAA Division II Coach of the Year?
A. Two (1987 and '90)

Q. What Northern Kentucky star was Great Lakes Valley Conference Player of the Year in 1989?
A. Derek Fields

Q. What Murray State star was Ohio Valley Conference Player of the Year in 1990 and '91?
A. Popeye Jones

Q. What two Louisville players were first-team All-Metro Conference selections in 1990?
A. Felton Spencer and LaBradford Smith

Q. Who was Western Kentucky's only All-OVC player in the Hilltoppers' final season in the league, 1982?
A. Craig McCormick

Q. What honor did Western Kentucky's Ed Diddle receive from the Kentucky Press Association in 1957?
A. Kentuckian of the Year

Q. Who captained UK's 1958 NCAA championship team?
A. Ed Beck

Q. Who was Kentucky's first All-American?
A. Basil Hayden (1921)

Q. Louisville's Denny Crum was accorded what statewide honor in 1990?
A. *Lexington Herald-Leader* Sportsman of the Decade

Q. What Louisville Cardinal was Metro Conference Player of the Year in 1987?
A. Herbert Crook

Q. What former Owensboro High School "Mr. Basketball" selection captained UK's 1964-65 team?
A. Randy Embry

Q. What national honor was accorded Western Kentucky coach Clem Haskins following the 1980-81 season?
A. NBC-TV Rookie Coach of the Year

Q. What UK guard won a Pan American Games gold medal as a member of the United States team in 1983?
A. Jim Master

Q. What Louisville Cardinal was Metro Conference Player of the Year in 1983?
A. Rodney McCray

Q. Who was Western Kentucky's first All-American?
A. Red McCrocklin (1938)

Q. What Kentucky Wesleyan All-American was named MVP of the 1966 NCAA Division II Tournament?
A. Sam Smith

Q. What UK player was named MVP of the 1984 NCAA Mideast Regional Tournament?
A. Dickey Beal

Q. Who won Kentucky's Freshman Leadership award in 1986?
A. Irving Thomas

Q. Who won or shared UK's Most Valuable Player award from 1965-67?
A. Pat Riley

Q. Who won UK's Leadership award in 1960 and '61?
A. Dick Parsons

Q. What two Louisville players were All-Missouri Valley Conference selections in 1969?
A. Butch Beard and Mike Grosso

Q. How many players did Western Kentucky place on the 1948 All-Kentucky Intercollegiate Athletic Conference (KIAC) team?
A. Five (Dee Gibson, Oran McKinney, John Oldham, Don Ray, Odie Spears; all were named to various All-American teams during their college careers)

Q. What Bellarmine star was Great Lakes Valley Conference Player of the Year in 1988?
A. Mike Holmes

Q. Who captained UK's 1975 NCAA runner-up team?
A. Jimmy Dan Conner

Q. What Murray State star was named OVC Player of the Year in 1969?
A. Claude Virden

Q. What year was Adolph Rupp elected to the Helms Foundation Hall of Fame?
A. 1944

Q. What Louisville All-American is the only player in NBA history to win Rookie of the Year and Most Valuable Player honors in the same season?
A. Wes Unseld (Baltimore Bullets, 1969)

Q. What Murray State coach earned OVC Coach of the Year recognition in 1977?
A. Fred Overton

Q. Who is UK's annual Most Assists award presented in honor of?
A. Claude Sullivan (a longtime Wildcat radio broadcaster)

Q. How many UK players were named to the 11-member Coaches' All-SEC team in 1993?
A. Two (Jamal Mashburn and Travis Ford; Mashburn was selected MVP)

Q. What Kentucky Wesleyan star was named NCAA Division II Player of the Year in 1991?
A. Corey Crowder

Q. What Murray State Racer was OVC Player of the Year in 1964?
A. Jim Jennings

Q. What UK standout was elected to the Naismith Basketball Hall of Fame in 1993?
A. Dan Issel

Q. What Eastern Kentucky player was a three-time All-OVC selection, 1964-66?
A. Eddie Bodkin

Q. Who co-captained Louisville's 1980 NCAA championship team?
A. Tony Branch and Darrell Griffith

Q. What former Shelby County High School "Mr. Basketball" selection was an Academic All-American at UK in 1971?
A. Mike Casey

Q. What Western Kentucky center earned All-American recognition in 1940 and '41?
A. Carlyle Towery

Q. What UK player was a unanimous selection for the All-SEC Freshmen Team in 1993?
A. Rodrick Rhodes (the only other unanimous selection on the five-player unit was Arkansas' Scotty Thurman)

Q. What UK legend was voted MVP of the 1948 and '49 NCAA Tournaments?
A. Alex Groza

Q. What year was Adolph Rupp inducted to the Naismith Basketball Hall of Fame?
A. 1969

Q. What UK transfer was an NCAA Division II All-American for Kentucky Wesleyan in 1957?
A. Mason Cope

Q. Who captained UK's 1946 NIT championship team?
A. Jack Parkinson

Q. What Murray State mentor was named OVC Coach of the Year in 1980 and '83?
A. Ron Greene

Q. Who is Louisville's only three-time All-American?
A. Wes Unseld (1966-68)

Q. What UK player was a first-team AP and UPI All-American in 1980?
A. Kyle Macy

Q. Who won UK's Outstanding Senior award in 1987?
A. James Blackmon

Q. Who captained UK's 1962 team?
A. Larry Pursiful

Q. What year was Ed Diddle inducted to the Naismith Basketball Hall of Fame?
A. 1971

Q. What Morehead State coach shared 1976 OVC Coach of the Year honors with Western Kentucky's Jim Richards?
A. Jack Schalow

Q. Who were tri-captains of UK's 1986 team?
A. Leroy Byrd, Roger Harden, Kenny Walker

Q. Who won UK's Mr. Deflection and Reggie Hanson Sacrifice awards in 1992?
A. Sean Woods

Q. What Morehead State star earned All-American recognition in 1950?
A. Sonny Allen

Q. What Western Kentucky center-forward earned All-OVC honors in 1960 and '61?
A. Charlie Osborne

Q. Who captained Louisville's 1956 NIT championship team?
A. Phil Rollins

Q. What year did Denny Crum coach the United States team in the Pan American Games?
A. 1987

Q. Who won UK's Leadership award in 1984?
A. Dickey Beal

Q. What UK junior was an AP first-team All-America selection in 1966?
A. Louie Dampier

Q. What UK player won a Pan American Games gold medal as a member of the United States team in 1975?
A. Rick Robey

Q. Who was the only Eastern Kentucky player selected to the 1970 All-OVC team?
A. Willie Woods

Q. Who was a three-time Academic All-SEC selection for Kentucky in the 1980s?
A. Chuck Verderber (1980-82)

Q. What Western Kentucky player was a first-team All-Sun Belt Conference selection in 1992?
A. Jack Jennings

Q. What year was Cliff Hagan inducted to the Naismith Basketball Hall of Fame?
A. 1977

Q. UK's Fewest Turnovers award is presented in honor of what key figure in Wildcat basketball history?
A. Harry C. Lancaster (Adolph Rupp's longtime assistant coach and a former UK athletics director)

Q. What year did UK retire the jersey of All-American Cotton Nash?
A. 1991

Q. Who was selected UK's Most Valuable Player in 1987?
A. Ed Davender

Q. What year were both Adolph Rupp and Ed Diddle elected to the Kentucky Athletic Hall of Fame?
A. 1964

Q. Who was captain of Adolph Rupp's first Kentucky team, 1930-31?
A. Carey Spicer

Q. Who won UK's Most Valuable Player award in 1963?
A. Ted Deeken

Q. What UK player won an Olympic Games gold medal as a member of the United States team in 1956?
A. Billy Evans

Q. Who was the only Morehead State player selected to the first All-OVC team in 1949?
A. Sonny Allen

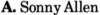

Q. What UK player won a Pan American Games silver medal as a member of the United States team in 1987?
A. Rex Chapman

Q. How many times did Western Kentucky's Bobby Rascoe earn All-OVC honors?
A. Three (1960-62)

Q. What year did Denny Crum coach the United States in the World University Games?
A. 1977

Q. What Morehead State standout was OVC Player of the Year in 1987?
A. Bob McCann

Q. What Western Kentucky star shared OVC Player of the Year honors with East Tennessee's Harley Swift in 1968?
A. Wayne Chapman

Q. What Murray State mentor was OVC Coach of the Year in 1992?
A. Scott Edgar

Q. Who is the only non-player or non-coach to have his "jersey" retired in Rupp Arena?
A. Cawood Ledford (1991)

Q. What two players were All-OVC selections for Morehead State in 1951?
A. Jack Baker and Don Miller

Q. What two Louisville players earned All-American recognition in 1975?
A. Junior Bridgeman and Allen Murphy

Q. Who was UK's first All-Southern Conference player?
A. Paul Jenkins (1926)

Q. Who was a consensus All-American for Kentucky in 1959?
A. Johnny Cox

Q. What year did Louisville's Denny Crum win his first Metro Conference Coach of the Year award?
A. 1979

Q. What Western Kentucky player earned the university's Male Athlete of the Year award in 1989?
A. Brett McNeal

Q. What Morehead State guard was an All-OVC selection in 1968 and '69?
A. Jerry Conley

Q. Who was honored as UK's "Fan of the Year" in 1990?
A. A. B. "Happy" Chander

Q. Who was a Helms Foundation All-American for Louisville in 1959?
A. Don Goldstein

Q. What year was Bellarmine's Joe Reibel named Great Lakes Valley Conference Coach of the Year?
A. 1991

Q. What UK broadcaster was named Kentucky Sportscaster of the Year in 1992?
A. Charlie McAlexander ("Charlie Mac" had previously been named top sportscaster in Mississippi (1975) and Tennessee (1990 and '91)

Q. What national news organizations and publications selected UK's Jamal Mashburn as a first-team All-American in 1993?
A. *Associated Press*, *Basketball Digest*, *Basketball Weekly*, Bob Gibbons, Dick Vitale, *NCAA Preview*, *Playboy*, *Street & Smith's*

Q. What UK player won an Olympic Games gold medal as a member of the United States team in 1960?
A. Adrian Smith

Q. What Louisville standout was Missouri Valley Conference Player of the Year in 1974 and '75?
A. Junior Bridgeman

Q. What Indiana University transfer was an All-OVC guard for Eastern Kentucky in 1981?
A. Tommy Baker

Q. What Kentucky Wesleyan coach was Great Lakes Valley Conference Coach of the Year in 1981, '83, and '84?
A. Mike Pollio

Q. What Morehead State star was OVC Player of the Year in 1963?
A. Harold Sergent

Q. What publication named Louisville's Denny Crum national Coach of the Year in 1983 and '86?
A. *The Sporting News*

Q. What Eastern Kentucky star was OVC Player of the Year in 1979?
A. James Tillman

Q. What year was Denny Crum inducted to the UCLA Athletic Hall of Fame?
A. 1990

Q. The road uniform of what Louisville player is on permanent display in the Naismith Basketball Hall of Fame at Springfield, Mass.?
A. Darrell Griffith

Q. What trio of UK players were named to the first All-SEC team in 1933?
A. Ellis Johnson, Forest Sale, John DeMoisey

Q. What pair of former Owensboro High School stars were NCAA Division II first-team All-Americans for Kentucky Wesleyan in 1984?
A. Rod Drake and Dwight Higgs

Q. What former UK assistant coach captained the Wildcats in 1961?
A. Dick Parsons

Q. What national honor did Kentucky Wesleyan coach Guy Strong receive in 1966?
A. NCAA Division II Coach of the Year (by the United States Basketball Writers Association)

Q. Who did UK broadcaster Cawood Ledford consider the best five Wildcat "sixth men" in his 39 years of calling games?
A. (in chronological order) Don Mills, James Lee, Jay Shidler, Deron Feldhaus, Richie Farmer

Q. Citizens Athletic Foundation and Converse selected what Louisville player an All-American in 1977?
A. Wesley Cox

Q. Who captained UK's "Fabulous Five" NCAA championship team of 1948?
A. Kenny Rollins

Q. What national Player of the Year award did Louisville's Darrell Griffith win in 1980?
A. John Wooden Award

Q. What year was UK's Eddie Sutton named national Coach of the Year by the Associated Press?
A. 1986

Q. What Indianapolis native was a UK All-American in 1935?
A. LeRoy Edwards

Q. What UK All-American was inducted to the Naismith Basketball Hall of Fame in 1981?
A. Frank Ramsey

Q. What Murray State standout was OVC Player of the Year in 1988 and '89?
A. Jeff Martin

Q. Former UK broadcaster Cawood Ledford holds the distinction of being the only person elected to what two Hall of Fames?
A. Kentucky Journalism and Kentucky Athletic

Q. What Western Kentucky mentor was named Sun Belt Conference Coach of the Year in 1987?
A. Murray Arnold

Q. What Eastern Kentucky guard was a three-time All-OVC selection, 1967-69?
A. Bobby Washington

Q. What two Western Kentucky players were named to the first All-OVC team in 1949?
A. John Oldham and Bob Lavoy

Q. Who is the only player in Kentucky Wesleyan history to win or share the team's Most Outstanding Player award four consecutive seasons?
A. Dwight Higgs (1981-84)

Q. What Eastern Kentucky coach was named OVC Coach of the Year in 1979?
A. Ed Byhre

Q. What Kentucky Wesleyan player was named Outstanding Player of the 1973 NCAA Division II Elite Eight Tournament?
A. Mike Williams

Q. What state players were invited to participate in the 1993 USA Basketball Team Trials?
A. Travis Ford (Kentucky); Dwayne Morton and Clifford Rozier (Louisville)

Q. Who did UK broadcaster Cawood Ledford name as the 10 best Wildcat players during his 39 years behind the microphone, 1953-92?
A. (in chronological order) Cliff Hagan, Frank Ramsey, Cotton Nash, Louie Dampier, Dan Issel, Kevin Grevey, Jack Givens, Kyle Macy, Sam Bowie, Kenny Walker

Q. When Sullivan Business College won the 1980 National Little College Athletic Association championship, what team member was named the tournament's Most Valuable Player?
A. Fred McKinney

CHAPTER 5

RECORDS

Q. Kentucky holds the national record for finishing in the top 10 of the Associated Press season-ending poll how many times?
A. 28 (North Carolina is second with 22 top 10 finishes)

Q. Who is Louisville's career assists leader?
A. LaBradford Smith (713)

Q. Who holds the Western Kentucky record for career steals?
A. Darnell Mee (279)

Q. What Louisville player holds the Metro Conference record for career free throw shooting?
A. Tony Branch (.901, 100 of 111)

Q. Who holds the UK record for three-pointers made in a season by a freshman?
A. Rex Chapman (68, in 176 attempts, 1986-87)

Q. Who holds the Murray State record for single-season free throw percentage?
A. Jimmy Young (.896, 86 of 96, 1969-70)

Q. Who holds the UK record for assists in a season by a freshman?
A. Dirk Minniefield (176, 1979-80)

Q. Kentucky holds the NCAA record for recording how many 30-victory seasons?
A. Seven (1948, 36 victories; 1947, 34; 1949, '51 and '86, 32; 1978 and '93, 30)

Q. What UK player was the NCAA Tournament leader in scoring average in 1992?
A. Jamal Mashburn (24 points per game for four games)

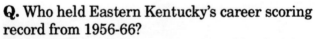

Q. Who held Eastern Kentucky's career scoring record from 1956-66?
A. Jack Adams (1,460 points; record broken by Eddie Bodkin, who finished with 1,507)

Q. What team set a Louisville record for victories in a season?
A. 1979-80 NCAA champions (33-3)

Q. Who holds the UK record for field goal attempts in a game?
A. Bill Spivey (42 - made 16 - vs. Georgia Tech, Feb. 18, 1950, at Lexington)

Q. What trio of players share the Louisville record for assists in a game with 12?
A. LaBradford Smith (three times), Henry Bacon, Keith Williams

Q. Kentucky set a Southeastern Conference record by hitting 76.5 percent of its field goal attempts in a 1981 game against what non-SEC opponent?
A. Notre Dame (UK won 34-28, Dec. 29, at Freedom Hall)

Q. Who holds the Morehead State single-game scoring record?
A. Brett Roberts (53 points, vs. Middle Tennessee, 1991-92)

Q. Who holds the Western Kentucky record for assists in a season?
A. James McNary (202, 1986-87)

Q. Who held UK's career scoring record from 1949 to 1964?
A. Alex Groza (1,744 points; Cotton Nash, who broke the record, scored 1,770)

Q. What Louisville player holds the Metro Conference record for minutes played in a season?
A. Billy Thompson (1,262, in 1984-85)

Q. Who broke Cliff Hagan's record for single-season scoring average (24.0, 1953-54) in 1968-69?
A. Dan Issel (26.6)

Q. What player holds the UK varsity record for points in a season by a freshman?
A. Rex Chapman (464, 1986-87)

Q. Who is Louisville's single-season steals leader?
A. Darrell Griffith (86, in 1979-80)

Q. Kentucky holds the NCAA record for producing how many 20-victory seasons?
A. 38

Q. What is the Louisville team record for free throws made in a game?
A. 44 (vs. Canisius, Dec. 10, 1955)

Q. What year did Western Kentucky set a school record for average home attendance?
A. 1970-71 (12,173 fans per game)

Q. What is the largest crowd to witness a Western Kentucky game?
A. 31,765 (Third-place game of the 1971 Final Four, Mar. 20, 1971, at the Houston Astrodome; WKU defeated Kansas 77-75)

Q. What state team holds the Ohio Valley Conference record for consecutive league championships won or shared?
A. Murray State (Five, 1988-92)

Q. What Louisville player established an NCAA record when he hit all 14 of his field goal attempts in a 1990 game against Southern Mississippi?
A. Cornelius Holden

Q. What state team holds the OVC record for consecutive losses in a season?
A. Morehead State (18, 1987-88)

Q. Who holds the Louisville record for career dunks?
A. Pervis Ellison (162)

Q. What Murray State player is the all-time scoring leader among Division I players in Kentucky?
A. Jeff Martin (2,484 points)

Q. What Morehead State player set an OVC record for consecutive free throws during the 1981-82 season?
A. Glenn Napier (46)

Q. What coach has won the most games at Eastern Kentucky?
A. Paul McBrayer (219)

Q. What is the lowest team field goal percentage ever shot in a game against Louisville?
A. .145 (10 of 69, by Georgetown College, Dec. 2, 1955)

Q. Kentucky Wesleyan holds the NCAA record for winning how many Division II national championships?
A. Six

Q. Who is the career scoring leader at Kentucky?
A. Dan Issel (2,138 points)

Q. What is the Louisville record for consecutive free throws made in a game?
A. 28 (vs. Indiana, Dec. 19, 1987, at Freedom Hall)

Q. What Western Kentucky star holds the OVC single-season scoring record?
A. Jim McDaniels (878 points, 1970-71)

Q. Who holds the Western Kentucky record for points in a game?

A. Clem Haskins (55, vs. Middle Tennessee, Jan. 30, 1965, at Diddle Arena)

Q. Who is the career leader in rebounds per game at Louisville?

A. Wes Unseld (18.9, 1966-68)

Q. Who holds the UK record for single-season field goal percentage?

A. Rick Robey (.635, 1977-78)

Q. What is the Louisville team record for steals in a game?

A. 21 (vs. Tulsa, Feb. 22, 1975, at Freedom Hall)

Q. What former Murray State legend set an NBA single-game scoring record that stood for 10 years?

A. Joe Fulks (playing for the Philadelphia Warriors, he scored 63 points against the Indianapolis Jets, Feb. 10, 1949)

Q. What Louisville player holds the Metro Conference record for career blocked shots?

A. Pervis Ellison (374)

Q. Who holds the Morehead State record for career rebounding average?

A. Steve Hamilton (16.1 per game)

Q. Who holds the record for career free throw percentage at Western Kentucky?
A. Charlie Osborne (.801, 511 of 638)

Q. Who is the all-time scoring leader at Kentucky Wesleyan?
A. Corey Crowder (2,282 points)

Q. What Morehead State player led the nation in scoring in 1991-92?
A. Brett Roberts (28.1 points per game)

Q. Who holds the Murray State record for field goal attempts in a game?
A. Bennie Purcell (45, vs. Kentucky Wesleyan, Jan. 19, 1952)

Q. What Western Kentucky player led the nation in field goal percentage during the 1958-59 season?
A. Ralph Crosthwaite (.645)

Q. Who is Morehead State's career scoring leader?
A. Herbie Stamper (2,072 points)

Q. Who is the UK record-holder for career three-point field goals made?
A. Derrick Miller (191, in 533 attempts, 1987-90)

Q. Who is UK's single-season record-holder for field goals made?
A. Dan Issel (369, in 667 attempts, 1969-70)

Q. What Louisville player holds the Metro Conference record for field goals made in a season?
A. Darrell Griffith (349, 1979-80)

Q. Who holds the Louisville record for points scored in a game?
A. Wes Unseld (45, vs. Georgetown College, Dec. 1, 1967, at Freedom Hall)

Q. Who holds the Louisville single-season record for rebound average?
A. Charlie Tyra (23.8 per game, 1955-56)

Q. Who holds the Kentucky Wesleyan record for career rebounds?
A. George Tinsley (1,115, 1966-69)

Q. Who holds the Eastern Kentucky record for consecutive free throws made?
A. Lee Lemos (28, 1964-65)

Q. Who holds the Western Kentucky record for career scoring average?
A. Jim McDaniels (27.6 points per game, 1969-71)

Q. What two UK teams share the national record for producing perfect seasons?
A. 1953-54 (25-0) and 1911-12 (9-0)

Q. What UK team set a school record for greatest scoring margin over opponents?
A. 1953-54 (the Wildcats UK by an average of 27.6 points per game)

Q. Who holds the UK varsity record for points in a game by a freshman?
A. Jamal Mashburn (31, vs. Georgia, Feb. 3, 1991, at Rupp Arena)

Q. What Western Kentucky team set a school record for games played in a season?
A. 1986-87 (38; won 29, lost 9)

Q. What is the Western Kentucky record for consecutive regular season victories?
A. 32 (Jan. 2, 1948 through Jan. 22, 1949; streak broken by Eastern Kentucky 42-40, Jan. 29, 1949, at Bowling Green)

Q. Who holds the Murray State record for career free throw percentage?
A. Greg Coble (.850, 147 of 173, 1989-91)

Q. Who holds the individual record for points scored in a game against Louisville?
A. Dave Corzine, of DePaul (46, Mar. 17, 1978)

Q. Who holds the UK record for career scoring average?
A. Dan Issel (25.7 points per game, 1968-70)

Q. What player scored the most points in a game against Kentucky?
A. Pete Maravich, of Louisiana State (64, Feb. 21, 1970, at Baton Rouge, La.)

Q. What Western Kentucky team set a school record for greatest scoring margin in a season?
A. 1942-43 (Western outscored its opponents by an average of 26.9 points per game)

Q. Who holds the record for career assists at Morehead State?
A. Howard Wallen (412)

Q. What team holds the Louisville record for blocked shots in a season?
A. 1982-83 (251 in 36 games)

Q. Who holds the Murray State single-game record for free throws attempted?
A. Howie Crittenden (28 - made 19 - vs. Western Kentucky, Feb. 25, 1955 in OVC Tournament, at Louisville)

Q. What year did UK set a school record for losses at home?
A. 1966-67 (seven)

Q. What state team holds the Ohio Valley Conference record for postseason appearances?
A. Western Kentucky (17; 9 NCAA, 8 NIT; the Hilltoppers departed the OVC after 34 seasons in 1982)

Q. What Louisville player holds the record for field goal percentage in a Metro Conference Tournament?
A. Derek Smith (.769, 1981)

Q. Who is the career scoring leader for Northern Kentucky?
A. Brady Jackson (1,980 points)

Q. What UK player holds the SEC record for rebounds in a season?
A. Bill Spivey (567 in 34 games, 1950-51)

Q. Who scored the most field goals in Western Kentucky history?
A. Jim McDaniels (935)

Q. Who holds the UK record for playing in the most SEC games?
A. Kenny Walker (72, 1983-86)

Q. What player committed the most personal fouls in UK history?
A. Mike Phillips (344, 1975-78)

Q. Who holds the Kentucky Wesleyan record for points scored in a game?
A. Mike Williams (51, vs. Austin Peay, Dec. 22, 1972, at Owensboro)

Q. What Eastern Kentucky guard is the OVC's career leader in assists?
A. Bruce Jones (699)

Q. Who holds the Louisville record for career field goal percentage?
A. Felton Spencer (.628)

Q. Who is Kentucky State's career scoring leader?
A. Travis Grant (4,045 points, national college leader)

Q. In what statistical category did Murray State's Popeye Jones lead the nation as a senior in 1991-92?
A. Rebounding (14.4 per game)

Q. Who held the Eastern Kentucky record for career rebounds from 1952-92?
A. Jim Beachtold (933; record broken by Mike Smith, who finished with 977)

Q. What Kentucky Wesleyan coach holds the school record for career winning percentage?
A. Wayne Chapman (.815, 128-29, from 1986-90)

Q. What is the largest crowd to witness a UK basketball game?
A. 64,151 (1993 Final Four semifinals, Louisiana Superdome, New Orleans; Michigan defeated UK 81-78 in overtime)

Q. UK holds the national record for appearing in how many NCAA Tournaments?
A. 34 (10 Final Fours)

Q. Louisville holds the NCAA record for producing how many consecutive winning seasons?
A. 46 (1945-90)

Q. Who holds the record for career free throws made at Kentucky?
A. Kenny Walker (550, in 733 attempts, 1983-86)

Q. Adolph Rupp established an NCAA record by winning how many games at Kentucky?
A. 876 (lost 190)

Q. Who holds the Western Kentucky record for single-season rebound average?
A. Rip Gish (15.5 per game, 1950-51)

Q. Who is Louisville's career scoring leader?
A. Darrell Griffith (2,333 points, 1977-80)

Q. What Morehead State player set an OVC record for single-season free throw percentage in 1974-75?
A. Mike Kelley (.915)

Q. Who holds the UK record for points scored in a game?
A. Dan Issel (53, vs. Mississippi, Feb. 7, 1970, at Oxford, Miss.)

Q. What is Kentucky's largest single-game margin of victory?
A. 77 points (143-66 vs. Georgia, Feb. 27, 1956, at Louisville)

Q. What Morehead State player established an OVC record when he hit all 17 of his free throw attempts in a 1966 game against Marshall?
A. Jim Sandfoss

Q. What season did Western Kentucky lead the nation in winning percentage?
A. 1947-48 (.933, 28-2 record)

Q. Who holds the Kentucky record for rebounds in a game?
A. Bob Burrow (34, vs. Temple, Dec. 10, 1955, at Lexington)

Q. Who is Kentucky's career leader in rebounds?
A. Dan Issel (1,078)

Q. Who holds the Louisville record for single-season rebound average?
A. Charlie Tyra (22.2 per game, 1955-56)

Q. Who holds the Morehead State record for single-season scoring average?
A. Dan Swartz (28.6 points per game, 1955-56)

Q. What team handed Western Kentucky its worst-ever defeat, Nov. 28, 1990?
A. Georgia (124-65, at Athens, Ga.)

Q. What season did UK lead the nation in scoring offense?
A. 1951-52 (82.3 points per game)

Q. UK averaged how many three-point field goals made per game to lead the nation in Rick Pitino's first season as coach, 1989-90?
A. 10 (281 in 28 games)

Q. How many times has Kentucky been the national leader in single-game scoring margin over opponents?
A. Five (1949, 24.3; 1951, 22.2; 1952, 26.9; 1954, 27.2; 1957, 14.8)

Q. What UK player set an NCAA Tournament record by hitting all 11 of his field goal attempts in UK's 1986 victory over Western Kentucky?
A. Kenny Walker

Q. What is the Murray State record for victories in a season?
A. 27 (1937-38)

Q. Who holds the Kentucky Wesleyan record for single-season scoring average?
A. Kelly Coleman (30.3 points per game, 1959-60)

Q. What is Western Kentucky's largest single-game margin of victory?
A. 96 points (103-7 over Adairville Independents in Ed Diddle's first game as Western coach, Jan. 20, 1923)

Q. Kentucky Wesleyan's George Tinsley holds the NCAA Division II record for being a starter on how many national championship teams?
A. Three (1966, '68, '69)

Q. What Kentucky State player was the NAIA leader in field goal percentage in 1974-75?
A. Gerald Cunningham (.681)

Q. What is the largest crowd to witness a Louisville basketball game?
A. 61,612 (vs. Georgetown in the Final Four semifinals, Mar. 27, 1982 at the Louisiana Superdome, New Orleans; Georgetown won 50-46)

Q. What Western Kentucky sophomore led the nation in field goal percentage in 1951-52?
A. Art Spoelstra (.516)

Q. What Kentucky Wesleyan player set an NCAA Division II record by hitting all nine of his three-point field goal attempts in a game against Wayne State, Mar. 14, 1992?
A. Steve Divine

Q. What team handed Louisville its worst-ever Freedom Hall defeat?
A. Kentucky (85-51, Dec. 27, 1986)

Q. Western Kentucky's Ed Diddle is the co-holder of what NCAA record with DePaul's Ray Meyer?
A. Most seasons coached at one school (42)

Q. Who holds the Eastern Kentucky record for career rebounds?
A. Mike Smith (977)

Q. What team handed Kentucky its worst-ever defeat?
A. Centre College (87-17, Jan. 28, 1910, at Danville)

Q. Who holds the Morehead State record for blocked shots in a game?
A. Ron Nicholson (12, vs. Toledo, 1971-72)

Q. What Louisville player led the nation in three-point field goal percentage in 1993?
A. Dwayne Morton (.531, 51 of 96; a U of L record)

Q. What team did UK defeat to become the first NCAA school to win 1,000 games?
A. Georgia (88-68, Jan. 13, 1969, at Lexington)

Q. What season did Morehead State lead the nation in scoring offense?
A. 1955-56 (95.9 points per game)

Q. Who holds the Eastern Kentucky record for career rebound average?
A. Garfield Smith (13.2 per game)

Q. Who is Eastern Kentucky's career scoring leader?
A. Antonio Parris (1,723 points)

Q. What Murray State center led the nation in rebounding in 1966-67?
A. Dick Cunningham (21.8 per game)

Q. Notre Dame's Austin Carr combined with what UK player to set an NCAA Tournament two-player, same-game scoring record in 1970?
A. Dan Issel (Carr - 52 points - and Issel - 44 - combined for 96 points in UK's 109-99 victory, Mar. 12, at Columbus, Ohio)

Q. What Morehead State player is the OVC's career leader in rebounds?
A. Steve Hamilton (1,675)

Q. Who holds the Western Kentucky record for rebounds in a game?
A. Tom Marshall (29, vs. Louisville, 1954)

Q. Who holds the UK record for single-season free throw percentage?
A. Larry Steele (.918, 1969-70)

Q. Who holds the UK career record for games played?
A. Ralph Beard (139, 1945-49)

Q. Who holds the Murray State and OVC record for career rebounding average?
A. Dick Cunningham (18.2 per game, 1966-68)

Q. Who holds the Louisville record for career games played?
A. Jeff Hall (145, 1983-86)

Q. Western Kentucky holds the OVC record for winning how many consecutive games in a season?
A. 21 (twice, 1953-54 and 1966-67)

Q. What Murray State player holds the OVC record for career free throws made and attempted?
A. Howie Crittenden (731 of 1,041, 1953-56)

Q. What Kentucky player led the 1949 NCAA Tournament in scoring average?
A. Alex Groza (27.3 points per game for three games)

Q. Who set a Morehead State record for field goals and field goal attempts in the same game?
A. Granville Williams (22 of 37, vs. Miami, Fla., 1961-62)

Q. What is the Louisville record for most turnovers in a game?
A. 38 (vs. Hawaii-Hilo, Dec. 20, 1984; U of L won, 80-75)

Q. Who holds the Western Kentucky record for field goal attempts in a game?
A. Darel Carrier (44, made 22, vs. Morehead State, Feb. 11, 1964, at Morehead)

Q. What is the UK team record for free throws made in a game?
A. 46 (53 attempts, vs. Vanderbilt, Jan. 7, 1963, at Nashville, Tenn.)

Q. Who holds the Louisville record for consecutive free throws made?
A. LaBradford Smith (36, 1987-88)

Q. What player holds the Rupp Arena record for points scored in a game?
A. David Robinson, of Navy (45, vs. Kentucky, Jan. 25, 1987; UK won, 80-69)

Q. Who is Kentucky's career leader in field goal percentage?
A. Charles Hurt (.593, 1980-83)

Q. Who holds the UK record for most consecutive free throws made?
A. Jim Master (40, 1981-82)

Q. Who holds the Eastern Kentucky record for scoring average in a season?
A. James Tillman (27.2 points per game, 1979-80)

Q. What coach holds the Kentucky Wesleyan record for career victories?
A. Robert Wilson (204)

Q. Who holds the Louisville record for field goal attempts in a season?
A. Darrell Griffith (631, 1979-80)

Q. What Morehead State player holds the OVC record for consecutive field goals made in a game?

A. Leonard Coulter (13, vs. Tennessee Tech, 1971-72)

Q. What state team holds the OVC record for rebounds in a season?

A. Western Kentucky (1,810, in 1953-54)

Q. What Morehead player shares the OVC record for rebounds in a game?

A. Steve Hamilton (38, vs. Florida State, 1956-57; also East Tennessee's Tommy Woods, vs. Middle Tennessee, 1964-65)

Q. What state player holds the NCAA Division II record for career field goals made?

A. Travis Grant, of Kentucky State (1,760; in 2,759 attempts, 1969-72)

Q. When Western Kentucky's Ed Diddle retired in 1964, what NCAA Division I coaching records did he hold?

A. Most victories (759), most games (1,061), most seasons (42)

Q. What UK player posted the top scoring average during the 1985 NCAA Tournament?

A. Kenny Walker (25 points per game for three games)

CHAPTER 6

ODDS & ENDS

Q. What was the irony of season-ending losses for Kentucky and Western Kentucky in 1993?
A. Both came in the NCAA Tournament, both were by 81-78 scores, and both were in overtime.

Q. Kentucky coach Adolph Rupp was born in what Kansas community?
A. Halstead

Q. In 30 seasons of play in Diddle Arena, what is Western Kentucky's won-lost record through 1993?
A. 319-90 (.779)

Q. Before joining the Louisville coaching staff in 1972, where was Jerry Jones an assistant coach for five seasons?
A. Pepperdine University

Q. What newspaper won a Pulitzer Prize in 1986 after publishing a series of 1985 stories detailing various alleged NCAA violations by the UK basketball program during the coaching reign of Joe B. Hall, 1972-85?
A. *Lexington Herald-Leader*

Q. UK players Fred Cowan, Larry Johnson and Dwane Casey graduated from what high school?
A. Union County

Q. What added significance to Western Kentucky's 71-67 victory over Tulane for the 1959 Sugar Bowl Tournament championship?
A. It was Ed Diddle's 700th men's basketball victory at Western.

Q. Former UK basketball coach Joe B. Hall accepted then rejected the head coach position at what school in 1969?
A. St. Louis University

Q. In five seasons during the late-'40s and early-'50s, where (other than Louisville) did UK play a "neutral site" home game in the state?
A. Owensboro Sportscenter (5-0 record)

Q. Western Kentucky's Physical Education Building (the "Big Red Barn") was renovated into what current campus facility in 1963?
A. Margie Helm Library

Q. What company provided Western Kentucky coach Ed Diddle with complimentary red towels during the latter stage of his life?
A. Cannon

Q. What was the front cover title of the May 29, 1989 edition of *Sports Illustrated*, which published a story on Kentucky's NCAA probation?
A. "Kentucky's Shame"

Q. Western Kentucky star Jim McDaniels graduated from what high school?
A. Allen County

Q. Prior to arriving at the University of Kentucky, where did Adolph Rupp coach four seasons of high school basketball?
A. Freeport, Illinois (67-16 record)

Q. On what Clay County, Ky. street does the family of Kentucky favorite Richie Farmer reside?
A. Richie Farmer Boulevard

Q. In a survey of college basketball coaches in 1990, Lexington's Rupp Arena was ranked second to what facility as the most difficult place in America for an opposing team to play?
A. Duke's Cameron Indoor Stadium

Q. Who scored on a baseline lay-in at the buzzer to give Western Kentucky a 76-75 victory over Austin Peay in the 1976 Ohio Valley Conference Tournament championship game?
A. Wilson James (at Diddle Arena; victory sent WKU to the NCAA Tournament for the first time since 1971)

Q. What injury did Kentucky's Mike Casey suffer following his junior season in 1969?
A. A crushed right leg (the result of a summer automobile accident)

Q. UK All-Americans Paul McBrayer and Forest Sale were graduates of what high school?
A. Kavanaugh (Lawrenceburg, Ky.)

Q. Various recruiting violations placed Western Kentucky on NCAA probation how many seasons in the 1970s?
A. Three (1972-73, 1973-74, 1974-75)

Q. What year did Louisville win its only National Invitation Tournament championship?
A. 1956

Q. Before moving into Freedom Hall in December, 1956, where did Louisville play its home games?
A. Jefferson County Armory (now Louisville Gardens)

Q. UK graduate Rex Chapman is a graduate of what high school?
A. Apollo

Q. What year did Kentucky win its first Southeastern Conference championship?
A. 1933 (the league's first year)

Q. What injury slowed Kentucky's Pat Riley in his senior season, 1966-67?
A. Two ruptured disks (occurred in water skiing accident at Herrington Lake, summer of '66)

Q. On what date did Shawnee High School's Tom Payne become the first African-American player to sign a basketball scholarship with Kentucky?
A. June 9, 1969

Q. What Frankfort facility is the home arena for Kentucky State University?
A. Farnham Dudgeon Civic Center (seating capacity, 7,200)

Q. What is the current seating capacity of Western Kentucky's E. A. Diddle Arena?
A. 11,300

Q. Kentucky's Travis Ford is a graduate of what high school?
A. Madisonville-North Hopkins

Q. As a player, UK's Joe B. Hall transferred to what school during the 1948-49 season?
A. Sewanee (University of the South)

Q. All-American Kyle Macy transferred to UK from what school?
A. Purdue

Q. What is the college alma mater of former Louisville coach Peck Hickman?
A. Western Kentucky

Q. What two state schools were ranked in the top five in the final Associated Press poll of 1949?
A. Kentucky (first) and Western Kentucky (fifth)

Q. What year did Lindsey Wilson College win the National Little College Athletic Association championship?
A. 1972

Q. Through 1976, what was the seating capacity of UK's Memorial Coliseum?
A. 11,500

Q. In what school did UK All-American Ralph Beard enroll after briefly leaving the University of Kentucky in the fall of his freshmen year, 1945?
A. University of Louisville

Q. In his 1975 book, *Basketball: The Dream Game in Kentucky,* who did sports writer Dave Kindred name to his All Kentucky college "Dream Team" starting five?
A. Kentucky's Ralph Beard and Western Kentucky's Dwight Smith (guards); Kentucky's Cliff Hagan and Dan Issel (forwards); and Kentucky's Bill Spivey (center)

Q. When was the last time Freedom Hall played host to the Final Four?
A. 1969 (UCLA, led by Lew Alcindor, defeated Purdue 92-72 for the title)

Q. What was the name of Western Kentucky's original basketball facility?
A. "Little Red Barn"

Q. UK All-American Cliff Hagan helped lead what team to the 1958 NBA championship?
A. St. Louis Hawks

Q. What was the portion of Lexington's Euclid Avenue that ran between UK's Memorial Coliseum and Stoll Field renamed in 1951?
A. "Avenue of Champions"
(in recognition of UK's 1950 Sugar Bowl football championship and its 1951 NCAA basketball championship)

Q. What is the home gymnasium for Kentucky's Union College?
A. Robinson Arena (seating capacity, 2,500)

Q. When was Louisville's final season as a member of the Missouri Valley Conference?
A. 1974-75

Q. What school did Western Kentucky star Wayne Chapman transfer from in 1964?
A. Kentucky

Q. Why was Western Kentucky's third-place finish in the 1971 Final Four vacated by the NCAA?
A. Hilltopper All-American Jim McDaniels signed an American Basketball Association professional contract early in his senior season. (Ironically, Villanova's runner-up finish to UCLA that year was also vacated, because Villanova All-American Howard Porter also signed a professional contract as an undergraduate.)

Q. What is the seating capacity of Bellarmine College's home gymnasium, Knight's Hall?
A. 3,200

Q. Who is credited with the longest field goal in Louisville basketball history?
A. Marv Selvy (70 feet, vs. Wichita State, Feb. 24, 1968)

Q. In 1944, UK coach Ed Diddle signed what twin cheerleaders from London, Ky. to four-year athletic scholarships?
A. Anna Jo and Betty Jo Cook (Western's basketball program had available scholarships, due to World War II.)

Q. Adrian Smith arrived at Kentucky after two years of stardom at what junior college?
A. Northeast Mississippi

Q. What is the current seating capacity of Louisville's Freedom Hall?
A. 18,865

Q. What basketball official called a controversial jump-ball foul on Western Kentucky's Greg Smith in the waning seconds of the Hilltoppers' 80-79 loss to Michigan in the 1966 NCAA Tournament at Iowa City, Iowa?
A. Steve Honzo

Q. What year did Murray State's Racer Arena open?
A. 1954

Q. What Georgia Tech player hit the game-winning shot when the Yellowjackets snapped UK's 129-game home winning streak, Jan. 8, 1955?
A. Joe Helms

Q. What team snapped Western Kentucky's 43-game Diddle Arena winning streak, Dec. 4, 1971?
A. Southwestern Louisiana (105-84)

Q. What team defeated UK in the 1985 NCAA Tournament, marking the end of the coaching reign of Joe B. Hall?
A. St. John's (86-70, at Denver)

Q. For whom was UK's Memorial Coliseum named?
A. Kentuckians killed in World War II

Q. What was the seating capacity of Western Kentucky's Physical Education Building, known as the "Big Red Barn"?
A. 4,500 (Western played there from 1931-63)

Q. What is the title of Louisville's basketball fight song?
A. "Fight U of L"

Q. What is the name of Northern Kentucky University's basketball facility?
A. Regents Hall (seating capacity, 2,500)

Q. On what date did the University of Kentucky hire Rick Pitino?
A. June 2, 1989

Q. What injury did Western Kentucky All-American Clem Haskins suffer late in his senior season, 1967?
A. Broken right (shooting) wrist (WKU, ranked third in America, was upset 75-69 by Murray State, Feb. 25, at Diddle Arena)

Q. Who hit the winning free throw in UK's 46-45 victory over Rhode Island in the 1946 NIT championship game?
A. Ralph Beard

Q. What team selected Kentucky's Vernon Hatton in the second round of the 1958 NBA Draft?
A. Cincinnati Royals

Q. What Louisville player missed a free throw that could have sealed victory in the Cardinals' 75-74 overtime loss to UCLA in the 1975 Final Four semifinals?
A. Terry Howard (who had made all 28 of his 1974-75 free throw attempts prior to that miss)

Q. What symbol of spirit is waved at games by Western Kentucky fans?
A. The Red Towel

Q. What future Western Kentucky starters helped lead Paducah Community College to the 1969 National Junior College championship?
A. Gary Sundmacker and Rex Bailey

Q. Besides Louisville, where did Denny Crum serve as a college head coach?
A. Pierce (Calif.) Junior College (1964-67)

Q. What is the seating capacity of Eastern Kentucky's McBrayer Arena?
A. 6,500

Q. Who made Dave Kindred's "Dream Team" second five from the book *Basketball: The Dream Game in Kentucky*?
A. Louisville's Jim Price and Murray State's Joe Fulks (guards), Kentucky's Frank Ramsey and Louisville's Charlie Tyra (forwards); and Kentucky's Alex Groza (center).

Q. What Western Kentucky player was a first round NBA draft choice of the Golden State Warriors in 1987?
A. Tellis Frank

Q. What was Kentucky's worst season during the Joe B. Hall era?
A. 1973-74 (13-13, 9-9 in SEC)

Q. What team defeated Kentucky in the 1989 SEC Tournament, marking the end of Eddie Sutton's Kentucky coaching career?
A. Vanderbilt (77-63, at Knoxville, Tenn.)

Q. What was the approximate cost to renovate Louisville's Freedom Hall in 1984?
A. $13.3 million

Q. What team did UK defeat in its first game in Alumni Gym?
A. Cincinnati (28-23, Dec. 13, 1924)

Q. What is the title of Western Kentucky's basketball fight song?
A. "Stand Up and Cheer!"

Q. What year did Kentucky adopt blue and white as its official colors?
A. 1892

Q. What UK player was selected in the fourth round of the 1983 NBA Draft by the Cleveland Cavaliers?
A. Derrick Hord

Q. What year did Cawood Ledford turn down an offer to broadcast University of Louisville football and basketball games?
A. 1973

Q. What is the single-game attendance record at Western Kentucky's Diddle Arena?
A. 14,277 (WKU vs. Murray State, Feb. 27, 1971; Western won, 73-59)

Q. Before being renovated in 1984, what was the seating capacity of Freedom Hall?
A. 16,613

Q. Who slam-dunked in the final seconds to put an exclamation point on Kentucky's NCAA championship game victory over Duke in 1978?
A. James Lee

Q. What team did Louisville defeat in Denny Crum's first home game as Cardinal coach, Dec. 4, 1971?
A. Bellarmine (116-58)

Q. What was Kentucky's record in Alumni Gym from 1924-50?
A. 262-25

Q. What is the title of UK's basketball fight song?
A. "On, On U of K!"

Q. What team selected Louisville's Rick Wilson in the second round of the 1978 NBA Draft?
A. Atlanta Hawks

Q. UK superstar Dan Issel graduated from what Illinois high school?
A. Batavia

Q. What three teams finished ahead of Kentucky in the final AP poll of 1964?
A. UCLA (first), Michigan (second), Duke (third)

Q. Who hit an off-balance jump shot with one second to play to give Louisville a 71-69 overtime victory over Kansas State in the 1980 NCAA Tournament?
A. Tony Branch

Q. What team did UK defeat to win the 1976 NIT championship?
A. North Carolina-Charlotte (71-67)

Q. Louisville's Bobby Turner starred at what Louisville high school?
A. Male

Q. On what date did Adolph Rupp die?
A. Dec. 10, 1977 (Ironically, UK defeated Rupp's alma mater, Kansas, that very evening by a 73-66 score at Lawrence, Kan.)

Q. Western Kentucky standout Harry Todd graduated from what high school?
A. Earlington

Q. Where did John Oldham coach before accepting the Western Kentucky job upon Ed Diddle's retirement in 1964?
A. Tennessee Tech

Q. What is the seating capacity of Rupp Arena?
A. 24,200

Q. Western Kentucky coach Murray Arnold was an assistant coach for what NBA team before accepting the WKU post in 1986?
A. Chicago Bulls

Q. Ed Diddle graduated from what Kentucky college?
A. Centre

Q. Western Kentucky's 1971 Final Four appearance was in what arena?
A. The Astrodome (Houston, Tex.)

Q. What year did the University of Kentucky first charge admission to men's games?
A. 1908 (25 cents)

Q. What Louisville player was selected by the Philadelphia 76ers in the first round of the 1989 NBA Draft?
A. Kenny Payne

Q. On what date did Ed Diddle die?
A. Jan. 2, 1970

Q. During the Rick Pitino era, what tune has been played in Rupp Arena when UK's starting lineup and coaching staff are introduced?
A. "Eye in the Sky" (by the Alan Parsons Project)

Q. What state school has the largest on-campus basketball facility?
A. Diddle Arena (11,300 seats)

Q. From what state high school did Louisville's Troy Smith graduate?
A. Fort Knox

Q. What is the seating capacity of Kentucky Wesleyan's home arena, the Owensboro Sportscenter?
A. 5,450

Q. Western Kentucky coach Ralph Willard was an assistant coach at what Big East school in 1986-87?
A. Syracuse

Q. From what college did former Murray State coach Steve Newton graduate?
A. Indiana State

Q. At what Louisville venue was the OVC Tournament held from 1964-66?
A. Convention Center

Q. Who hit two free throws with no time on the clock to give Eastern Kentucky a controversial 78-77 victory over Western Kentucky in the 1979 OVC Tournament championship game at Richmond?
A. Dave Tierney (subsequently, video tapes showed that Tierney was fouled about 3.5 seconds after the final buzzer)

Q. Who were the two officials calling the 1979 OVC Tournament championship game between Eastern and Western?
A. Ralph Stout and Burrell Crowell

Q. What is the name of UK's basketball dormitory?
A. Wildcat Lodge (formerly Joe B. Hall Wildcat Lodge)

Q. Travis Ford transferred to Kentucky from what school?
A. Missouri

Q. What team defeated Western Kentucky in the Hilltoppers' final game as a member of the OVC, 1982?
A. Purdue (72-65 in the first round of the NIT, at West Lafayette, Ind.)

Q. From what Texas high school did Louisville star LaBradford Smith graduate?
A. Bay City

Q. What year did Ralph Hacker join Cawood Ledford as color analyst for the UK Basketball Network?
A. 1972

Q. Gene Keady departed Western Kentucky in 1980 to accept what Big Ten Conference coaching post?
A. Purdue

Q. In what arena did Kentucky defeat Duke for the 1978 NCAA championship?
A. The Checkerdome (St. Louis, Mo; facility is now named The Arena)

Q. What team selected Kentucky Wesleyan's Kelly Coleman in the second round of the 1960 NBA Draft?
A. New York Knicks

Q. What is the name of Western Kentucky's basketball dormitory?
A. Diddle Hall (formerly Diddle Dorm)

Q. What was Cawood Ledford's first season as play-by-play radio broadcaster for UK games?
A. 1953-54

Q. What legend of the game coached Adolph Rupp at Kansas?
A. Phog Allen

Q. Who made a short jump shot with three seconds to play to give Ohio State an 82-81 upset victory over Kentucky in the 1968 NCAA Tournament?

A. Dave Sorenson (game was played at Lexington's Memorial Coliseum)

Q. What team did Kentucky defeat 75-6 in a game played Jan. 8, 1945?

A. Arkansas State

Q. Who is credited with the longest field goal in UK basketball history?

A. Cliff Barker (63 feet, 7 inches, vs. Vanderbilt, Feb. 26, 1949 in Alumni Gym)

Q. What team drafted UK players Jerry Bird and Phil Grawemeyer in the third round of the 1956 NBA Draft?

A. Minneapolis Lakers

Q. What academic year was UK's "Wildcat" mascot originated?

A. 1976-77

Q. Western Kentucky coach Ralph Willard is a graduate of what college?

A. Holy Cross

Q. In what Kentucky town was Ed Diddle born?

A. Gradyville (Adair County)

Q. What team did UK defeat in the Wildcats'
final game in Memorial Coliseum?
A. Mississippi State (94-93, Mar. 8, 1976)

Q. What season did Cawood Ledford become the
lone radio voice of the Kentucky Wildcats'
basketball team?
A. 1967-68

Q. While coaching UK games, what three good
luck charms did Adolph Rupp carry in his
pocket?
A. A buckeye, rabbit's foot and four-leaf clover

Q. Following the 1988-89 season, UK's LeRon
Ellis transferred to what school?
A. Syracuse

Q. From Feb. 5, 1949 to Jan. 6, 1955, Western
Kentucky won 67 consecutive home games.
What team ended the streak?
A. Xavier of Ohio (82-80 in overtime, Jan. 10,
1955)

Q. What was UK's first season of college
basketball?
A. 1903 (1-2 record)

Q. What was the only team ranked ahead of
Louisville in the final AP and UPI polls of 1983?
A. Houston

Q. What was the first season Louisville drew over 200,000 spectators to Freedom Hall?
A. 1976-77 (203,248 for 16 home games)

Q. Why are Western Kentucky's teams known as "Hilltoppers"?
A. Western's campus - known as "the Hill" - has a summit that rises 232 feet above nearby Barren River.

Q. During what season did UK record its first 100-point game?
A. 1950-51 (Kentucky defeated Tulane 104-68, Jan. 29, 1951, at New Orleans)

Q. What team did Kentucky defeat to win the 1951 NCAA championship?
A. Kansas State (68-58, at Minneapolis, Minn.)

Q. What is the only year Murray State finished among the nation's top 20 teams in the final Associated Press poll?
A. 1951 (16th)

Q. Who hit a 48-foot shot with 12 seconds to play, giving Kentucky a 35-33 victory over Marquette, Feb. 14, 1938 (at Alumni Gym)
A. Joe Hagan

Q. John Mauer, Adolph Rupp's predecessor, left Kentucky to coach basketball at what SEC school?
A. Tennessee

Q. What Wildcat hit a baseline jump shot at the buzzer to force overtime in the UK-Louisville "Dream Game" of the 1983 NCAA Tournament?
A. Jim Master

Q. During what academic year was the "Hilltoppers" nickname established at Western Kentucky?
A. 1925-26

Q. What team selected UK's Jimmy Dan Conner in the second round of the 1975 NBA Draft?
A. Phoenix Suns

Q. Ed Diddle arrived at Western Kentucky in 1922 after coaching basketball at what Kentucky high school for two seasons?
A. Greenville

Q. What was the first team to defeat an Ed Diddle-coached men's basketball team at Western Kentucky?
A. Centre (Diddle's alma mater, 26-20, Jan. 17, 1923, at Danville)

Q. Why did the 1974 Morehead State at Illinois State encounter come to be known as "The "Missing Six" game?
A. Morehead coach Bill Harrell, with four consecutive OVC games following the Illinois State contest, chose to leave his top six players at home. Illinois State, which won 113-74, cried fraud. It was Harrell's last year as Morehead's coach.

Q. What season did Murray State score 100 points in a game for the first time?
A. 1949-50 (Murray defeated Middle Tennessee 100-59, Feb. 4, 1950, at Murray)

Q. What team defeated Kentucky in the 1972 NCAA Tournament, marking the end of Adolph Rupp's 41-year reign as Wildcat coach?
A. Florida State (73-54, at Dayton, Ohio)

Q. During what academic year did Western Kentucky's mascot "Big Red" debut?
A. 1979-80 (conceived, designed and built by WKU student Ralph Carey who was the first "Big Red")

Q. What state school won three consecutive National Little College Athletic Association championships from 1967-69?
A. Sullivan Business College

Q. Former UK star Dwight Anderson transferred to what school?
A. Southern California

Q. What is the name of the complex in which Louisville's Freedom Hall is housed?
A. Kentucky Fair and Exposition Center

Q. Morehead State coach Dick Fick was an assistant coach at what school from 1985-91?
A. Creighton

CHAPTER 7

THE WOMEN'S GAME

Q. What team did Western Kentucky defeat in the second round of the 1993 NCAA Tournament?
A. Miami, Fla. (78-63, at Diddle Arena)

Q. Who has been Northern Kentucky's coach since 1983?
A. Nancy Winstel

Q. What team did Kentucky defeat in the third round of the 1982 NCAA Tournament?
A. South Carolina (73-69)

Q. What Western Kentucky player was named Most Valuable Player of the 1991 Sun Belt Conference Tournament?
A. Mary Taylor

Q. What number was worn by Murray State star Laura Lynn?
A. 32

Q. Who set a Kentucky Wesleyan record for single-season scoring average in 1991-92?
A. Octavia Dean (22.2 points per game)

Q. Who is Murray State's career scoring leader?
A. Sheila Smith (2,287 points)

Q. Who was the first "Miss Basketball" selection from Kentucky to sign with UK during the coaching reign of Sharon Fanning?
A. Becky McKinley (of Bullitt East High School, 1992)

Q. What team did Western Kentucky defeat to win the 1993 Sun Belt Conference Tournament championship game?
A. Louisiana Tech (81-73, at Ruston, La.)

Q. Who coached Morehead State from 1976-84?
A. Mickey Wells (156-91 record)

Q. What 1920s Western Kentucky all-state forward later married her coach, Ed Diddle?
A. Louise Monin

Q. What two Kentucky players were selected to the first all-University of Kentucky Invitational Tournament team in 1980?
A. Patty Jo Hedges and Liz Lukschu

Q. What is the Western Kentucky record for victories in a season?
A. 32 (1985-86; four losses)

Q. What Murray State player led the Ohio Valley Conference in rebounding in 1991-92?
A. Fondoelyn Garner (11 per game)

Q. What two teams did Western Kentucky defeat to win the Cahill Invitational tournament at Jamaica, N.Y., 1987-88?
A. Oregon (83-71) and St. John's (84-67)

Q. Who became Morehead State's coach in 1992?
A. Janet Gabriel

Q. Who was Morehead State's coach in 1970-71?
A. Carole Stewart (5-3 record)

Q. Who became Murray State's coach in 1991?
A. Kelly Breazeale (resigned following 1992-93 season)

Q. Who holds the Kentucky Wesleyan record for rebounds in a game?
A. Janice Johnson (24, vs. Georgetown College, Feb. 5, 1979)

Q. Who led Eastern Kentucky in scoring during the 1991-92 season?
A. Angie Cox (16.8 points per game)

Q. In Western Kentucky's Final Four season of 1992, what was the Lady Toppers' record after eight games?
A. 4-4 (finished 27-8)

Q. When was Terry Hall's final season as UK coach?
A. 1986-87 (17-11 record)

Q. What team eliminated Western Kentucky in the 1986 Final Four semifinals?
A. Texas (90-65, at Rupp Arena)

Q. Who holds the Murray State career record for rebounds per game?
A. Jackie Mounts (13.1)

Q. Louisville coach Bud Childers played basketball at what Southeastern Conference school in 1974-75?
A. Mississippi State

Q. What was the nickname of Western Kentucky player Melinda Carlson?
A. "Bird"

Q. Who holds the Louisville record for points scored in a game?
A. Erica Washington (37, vs. Murray State, Dec. 6, 1980)

Q. What Western Kentucky star was a member of the 1992 Final Four all-tournament team?
A. Kim Pehlke

Q. When was the last time Centre College reached the NCAA Division III Final Four?
A. 1990

Q. What was Western Kentucky ranked in the final Associated Press poll of 1985?
A. 14th

Q. Who holds Morehead State's single-game scoring record?
A. Donna Murphy (37 points, vs. Murray State, 1979-80)

Q. What team defeated Louisville in the second round of the 1993 NCAA Tournament?
A. Auburn (66-61, at Auburn, Ala.)

Q. Through 1993, when was the only season Western Kentucky appeared in the National Women's Invitational Tournament?
A. 1983-84

Q. Who led Murray State in scoring and rebounding in 1981 and '82?
A. Diane Oakley

Q. What team defeated Western Kentucky in the Lady Toppers' first NCAA Final Four appearance, 1985?
A. Georgia (91-78 in semifinals, at Austin, Tex.)

Q. Who coached Eastern Kentucky to a 20-9 record in 1991-92?
A. Larry Inman

Q. At what state school did Louisville's Bud Childers begin his collegiate coaching career?
A. Cumberland College (49-10 record in two seasons, 1982 and '83)

Q. What Western Kentucky player was MVP of the 1988 Sun Belt Conference Tournament?
A. Susie Starks

Q. What was the nickname of former Louisville star Nell Knox?
A. "Sweet Nell"

Q. Who is Murray State's only unanimous three-time All-OVC selection?
A. Laura Lynn (1979-81)

Q. What Morehead State star was named OVC Player of the Year in 1980?
A. Donna Murphy

Q. Who paced Western Kentucky in scoring in the Lady Toppers' NCAA championship game loss to Stanford in 1992?
A. Liesa Lang (18 points)

Q. Who holds the Kentucky Wesleyan record for single-season field goal percentage?
A. Connie Logsdon (.634, 1986-87)

Q. Who holds the Louisville record for steals per game in a season?
A. Gwen Doyle (3.38, 1991-92)

Q. In Paul Sanderford's first 10 seasons at Western Kentucky (1983-92) the Lady Toppers won what percentage of their games in Diddle Arena?
A. 92 percent (144-12)

Q. What Murray State star was selected OVC Player of the Year in 1984?
A. Karen Hubert

Q. What was Western Kentucky's first season of women's college basketball?
A. 1914-15 (1-0 record)

Q. What is the Louisville team record for points scored in a game?
A. 109 (vs. Appalachian State, 61, Feb. 23, 1991

Q. Who coached Western Kentucky to consecutive 22-9 seasons, 1977 and '78?
A. Julia Yeater

Q. What Kentucky star was a Kodak All-American in 1982 and '83?
A. Valerie Still

Q. How many Murray State players were named to the first All-OVC team in 1979?
A. Three (Laura Lynn, Cindy Barrix, Jackie Mounts)

Q. By what score did Western Kentucky defeat Alabama in the first round of the 1992 NCAA Tournament?
A. 98-68 (at Diddle Arena)

Q. What was the record of Sullivan College in 1992-93?
A. 31-1

Q. Who hit a last-second shot to give Western Kentucky a 92-90 upset victory over undefeated and No. 1 Texas in the 1985 NCAA Mideast Regional championship game?
A. Lillie Mason (at Diddle Arena; victory denied Texas a spot in the Final Four on their home court in Austin)

Q. Who was the only Murray State player selected to the 1981 All-OVC team?
A. Laura Lynn

Q. Who holds the career rebounding record at Northern Kentucky?
A. Peggy Vincent (1,166)

Q. Who coached Kentucky Wesleyan to a 21-7 record in 1991-92?
A. Scott Lewis

Q. What Morehead State star was selected OVC Player of the Year in 1983?
A. Priscilla Blackford

Q. Who was a first-team All-Metro Conference selection for Louisville in 1993?
A. Nell Knox

Q. Who holds the Murray State record for points scored in a game at Racer Arena?
A. Sheila Smith (38 points, three times; vs. Ohio University, Nov. 28, 1988; vs. Morehead State, Jan. 18, 1988; vs. Morehead State, Feb. 27, 1989)

Q. What team did Western Kentucky defeat to win the women's college basketball state championship in 1923?
A. Kentucky (27-19; Western coached by Ed Diddle; UK coached by A. B. "Happy" Chandler)

Q. What Eastern Kentucky player was an All-OVC selection in 1991?
A. Kelly Cowan

Q. What pair of Louisville players were All-Metro Conference Tournament selections in 1980?
A. Joan Dunaway·and Janet McNew

Q. Through 1993, how many 20-victory seasons had Western Kentucky coach Paul Sanderford produced in 11 years at the school?
A. 10

Q. What Eastern Kentucky player set an OVC record for steals in a season in 1990-91?
A. Angie Cox (105)

Q. What is the highest ranking Western Kentucky has achieved in the final AP poll?
A. Fifth (1986)

Q. In 1989, coach Bud Childers arrived at Louisville from what state school?
A. Murray State

Q. Who holds the Western Kentucky record for field goals and field goals attempted in a game?
A. Brenda Chapman (19 of 31, vs. Murray State, 1977-78)

Q. What is Morehead State's largest margin of defeat?
A. 50 points (Eastern Kentucky 78, Morehead State 28, in 1974-75 season)

Q. What is Western Kentucky's longest winning streak in a season?
A. 21 games (1990-91)

Q. Who was the first Louisville player to score 30 or more points in a game?
A. Audrey Baines (30, vs. Morehead State, Jan. 11, 1979)

Q. Who holds the Murray State record for points scored in a game?
A. Karen Johnson (40, vs. Tennessee Tech, Jan. 25, 1988)

Q. Who holds the Western Kentucky career record for rebound average?
A. Donna Doellman (8.4 per game)

Q. Who is Kentucky's career leader in rebounding?
A. Valerie Still (1,525)

Q. Who is Morehead State's career leader in rebounding?
A. Donna Murphy (1,442)

Q. What distinction did Western Kentucky stars Clemette Haskins and Kim Pehlke share?
A. Both wore number 21 at WKU

Q. How many times was Valerie Still named All-American by *Street & Smith* magazine?
A. Three (1981-83)

Q. What Western Kentucky standout was named Most Valuable Player of the 1992 NCAA Mideast Regional Tournament?
A. Kim Pehlke

Q. Who holds the Louisville record for rebounds in a game?
A. Troya Landrum (23, vs. Morehead State, Dec. 30, 1988)

Q. Who holds the Kentucky Wesleyan record for assists in a game?
A. Brenda Brit (15, vs. Indiana Tech, Dec. 30, 1982)

Q. Who led UK in scoring in 1986-87?
A. Bebe Croley (17.7 points per game)

Q. What former Western Kentucky player is the only athlete (man or woman) to compete in the NCAA's Final Four for two teams?
A. Debbie Scott (1992 for WKU; 1990 for Tennessee)

Q. What team defeated Western Kentucky in the 1992 NCAA Tournament championship game?
A. Stanford (78-62, at the Sports Arena, Los Angeles)

Q. Through 1993, what was Kentucky's all-time record versus Tennessee?
A. 5-24

Q. Who holds the Murray State record for rebounds in a game?
A. Jackie Mounts (28, vs. Vanderbilt, Nov. 30, 1977)

Q. Who coached Louisville from 1976-80?
A. Terry Hall (79-54 record)

Q. What year did Louisville win its first Metro
Conference regular season championship?
A. 1992 (11-1 in Metro; 20-9 overall)

Q. Who is Morehead State's career leader in
assists?
A. Irene Moore (499)

Q. Before arriving at Western Kentucky in 1982,
where did Paul Sanderford coach?
A. Louisburg (N.C.) Junior College (163-19
record in six seasons)

Q. Who holds the Murray State career record for
steals?
A. Julie Pinson (242)

Q. When was the last time Kentucky was
ranked in the final AP poll?
A. 1983 (12th)

Q. Who is the career scoring leader at Northern
Kentucky?
A. Peggy Vincent (1,883 points)

Q. What was the only team to defeat Western
Kentucky at Diddle Arena during the Lady
Toppers' Final Four season of 1991-92?
A. Kentucky (67-66)

Q. Who is the only Western Kentucky player to earn first-team Kodak All-American honors?
A. Lillie Mason (1985)

Q. What is the best single-season won-lost record in Morehead State history?
A. 28-4 (.875, 1978-79)

Q. Who holds the Kentucky record for rebound average in a season?
A. Pam Browning (16.8 per game, 1974-75)

Q. Who holds the Western Kentucky record for single-season field goal percentage?
A. Dianne Depp (.598, 1980-81)

Q. What three Morehead State players were named to the All-OVC team in 1979?
A. Donna Murphy, Donna Stephens, Michelle Stowers

Q. Who coached Murray State from 1971-77?
A. Dew Drop Rowlett (59-68 record)

Q. Who is Western Kentucky's career scoring leader?
A. Lillie Mason (2,262 points)

Q. What is the nickname of Bellarmine College?
A. Belles

Q. What Eastern Kentucky player holds the OVC record for single-season free throw percentage?
A. Lisa Gooden (.913, 137-150, in 1982-83)

Q. Who holds the UK record for rebounds in a game?
A. Valerie Still (27, vs. National College, Feb. 9, 1982)

Q. Who coached Brescia College to consecutive 24-victory seasons, 1989 and '90?
A. Lee Buchanan

Q. What year did Louisville produce its first 20-victory season?
A. 1982-83 (20-10)

Q. Who holds the Western Kentucky record for career steals?
A. Clemette Haskins (285)

Q. Who coached Murray State to its only 20-victory seasons in 1988 and '89?
A. Bud Childers (21-7 in '88, 22-10 in '89)

Q. What team did Western Kentucky defeat in the semifinals of the 1992 Final Four?
A. Southwest Missouri State (82-72, at Los Angeles)

Q. What year did UK set a school record for single-game attendance average?
A. 1982-83 (3,645 per game)

Q. Who holds the Kentucky Wesleyan record for points scored in a game?
A. Octavia Dean (37, twice; vs. Lewis, Jan. 25, 1992, vs. Bellarmine, Mar. 7, 1992)

Q. Who led Morehead State in rebounding three consecutive seasons, 1990-92?
A. Julie Magrane

Q. Who is UK's career leader in assists?
A. Patty Jo Hedges (731)

Q. What UK star earned *Street & Smith's* magazine All-American recognition in 1977?
A. Pam Browning

Q. How many seasons did Ed Diddle coach Western Kentucky's women's basketball team?
A. Two (1923 and '24, 11-6 record)

Q. What team won the Kentucky Women's Intercollegiate Conference (KWIC) Tournament in 1976?
A. Eastern Kentucky (defeated Western Kentucky 81-71 in championship game, at Lexington)

Q. Who is Louisville's career leader in assists per game?
A. Stephanie Edwards (5.8)

Q. What number was worn by Kentucky star Leslie Nichols?
A. 11

Q. Who holds the Murray State record for blocked shots in a game?
A. Jeannie Pollman (9, vs. Tennessee-Chattanooga, Dec. 1, 1987)

Q. Who preceded Paul Sanderford as coach at Western Kentucky?
A. Eileen Canty

Q. Who earned UK's Most Valuable Player honors in 1988 and '89?
A. Jodie Whitaker

Q. What was Bud Childers' best won-lost record in five seasons as coach at Murray State?
A. 21-7 (.750, in 1987-88)

Q. How many times was UK's Leslie Nichols named to the All-SEC team?
A. Three (1984-86)

Q. What Morehead state player holds the OVC record for consecutive free throws made?
A. Kelly Stamper (27, 1986-87)

Q. What is the home arena of the University of Kentucky Lady Kats?
A. Memorial Coliseum (revised seating capacity, 8,700)

Q. Who is the only Murray State player to record a triple-double in a game?
A. Karen Johnson (19 points, 12 rebounds, 10 assists, vs. Ill.-Chicago, Dec. 17, 1987)

Q. What is the highest ranking UK has achieved in the final AP poll?
A. 11th (1981)

Q. Who is Western Kentucky's career leader in assists?
A. Clemette Haskins (731)

Q. Who were UK's tri-captains in 1978-79?
A. Linda Edelman, Debbie Mack, Debra Oden

Q. What was the nickname of Western Kentucky star Lillie Mason?
A. "Magic"

Q. Who is Morehead State's single-season assists leader?
A. Teresa Ruby (193, 1984-85)

Q. In nine seasons as Louisville coach, what was Peggy Fiehrer's best won-lost record?
A. 19-8 (1981-82)

Q. In seven seasons as Kentucky coach, how many 20-victory seasons did Terry Hall produce?
A. Three

Q. What organization selected Western Kentucky's Clemette Haskins a first-team All-American in 1987?
A. Naismith

Q. What former UK Lady Kat was a Kentucky "Miss Basketball" selection at Owensboro Catholic High School?
A. Kris Miller

Q. What Western Kentucky player set a school record by hitting all 13 of her free throws in a 1988 game?
A. Tandreia Green (vs. Ohio University)

Q. Through 1993, what was Sharon Fanning's best season as UK coach?
A. 1989-90 (23-8)

Q. Who holds the Kentucky Wesleyan record for career three-point field goal percentage?
A. Stacy Calhoun (.368, 99 of 269)

Q. What two players hold the Western Kentucky record for rebounds in a game?
A. Brigette Combs and Tandreia Green (20, in the same game, vs. West Virginia, Mar. 15, 1989)

Q. Who led Murray State in steals three consecutive seasons, 1980-82?
A. Bridgette Wyche

Q. What number was worn by Western Kentucky's Lillie Mason?
A. 32 (retired by school)

Q. What is the largest Diddle Arena crowd for a women's basketball game?
A. 12,951 (WKU defeated Old Dominion 74-64, Feb. 23, 1986; at the time, this was the second-largest crowd to witness a women's college basketball game)

Q. Since 1975-76, in how many home arenas has Louisville played its games?
A. 10 (Freedom Hall, Ballard High, Bellarmine College, Broadbent Arena, Butler High, Commonwealth Convention Center, Spalding University, Student Activities Center, Thomas Jefferson High, Manual High)

Q. What number was worn by Morehead State standout Donna Murphy?
A. 44

Q. Who holds the Louisville record for single-season free throw percentage?
A. Rosalind Smith (.825, 1980-81)

Q. UK set an NCAA record with a Memorial Coliseum crowd of 10,622, Feb. 5, 1983. Who was the Lady Kats' opponent?
A. Old Dominion (UK won, 80-66)

Q. What three Morehead State players are members of the university's Athletic Hall of Fame?
A. Donna Murphy, Donna Stephens, Debra Ames

Q. Who is Western Kentucky's career rebounding leader?
A. Lillie Mason (1,002)

Q. What number was worn by UK standout Valerie Still?
A. 12

Q. What two Western Kentucky players earned Academic All-American honors in 1981?
A. Laurie Heltsley and Alicia Polson

Q. Who led Murray State in field goal percentage four consecutive seasons, 1988-91?
A. Michelle Wenning

Q. In four seasons as UK coach, what was Debbie Yow's best year?
A. 1979-80 (24-5)

Q. What Kodak Junior College All-American did Western Kentucky sign at the conclusion of the 1992-93 season?
A. Michelle Reed (of Sullivan College)

Q. What former Tennessee Kodak All-American now coaches at Centre College?
A. Cindy Noble-Hauserman

Q. Who holds the Morehead State record for career free throw percentage?
A. Kelly Downs (.826)

Q. What is the Murray State team record for points scored in a game?
A. 117 (vs. Elizabethtown Community College 42, Dec. 8, 1977)

Q. What former Kentucky Wildcat guard coached Kentucky Wesleyan to a 17-1 record in 1978-79?
A. Randy Embry

Q. What number was worn by Western Kentucky star Renee Westmoreland?
A. 4

Q. Transylvania signed what Paris High School star at the conclusion of the 1992-93 season?
A. Megan May

Q. What team did Kentucky defeat to win the championship game of the Nevada-Reno New Year's Classic, Dec. 29, 1989?
A. Indiana (78-71)

Q. Who holds the Northern Kentucky record for career field goal percentage?
A. Linda Honigford (.540)

Q. What is Morehead State's largest margin of victory in a game?
A. 63 points (MSU 115, West Virginia State 52, 1986-87 season)

Q. What Morehead State player led the OVC in free throw percentage in 1991-92?
A. Sherita Joplin (.845, 71 of 84)

Q. What season did Kentucky defeat Tennessee for the first time?
A. 1978-79 (66-64, at Lexington)

Q. In Louisville's first 100-point game, who did the Lady Cards defeat?
A. Evansville (101-47, Jan. 22, 1977, at Louisville's Butler High School)

Q. Who coached Western Kentucky to a 19-7 record in 1975-76?
A. Dr. Carol Hughes

Q. In Western Kentucky's first 100-point game, the Lady Toppers defeated what state team?
A. Louisville (102-57, first game of 1975-76 season)

Q. What is the only season UK failed to average at least 1,000 fans per home game during the 1980s?
A. 1987-88 (837 per game)

Q. What UK standout hit all 10 of her field goal attempts in a game against Louisiana State, Mar. 3, 1984?
A. Lisa Collins

Q. Through 1993, what was Murray State's record in games played against Western Kentucky?
A. 10-20

Q. Who led UK in scoring in 1991-92?
A. Stacy McIntyre (16.1 points per game)

Q. Through 1993, how many Ohio Valley Conference regular season championships had Eastern Kentucky, Morehead State and Murray State won or shared?
A. None

Q. What is the Western Kentucky team record for points scored in a game?
A. 126 (vs. Western Carolina, 1990-91 season, at Diddle Arena)

Additional titles from
McClanahan Publishing House
Inc.

Crazy About the Cats, From Rupp to Pitino
Dining in Historic Kentucky
Dining in Historic Georgia
Dining in the Historic South
Savor Lake Superior
Nuts About Pecans
On Bended Knees: The Night Rider Story
Kentucky's Thomas D. Clark
Cooking With Curtis Grace
Cook Talk With Curtis Grace and Friends
A Little Touch of Grace

KENTUCKY COLLEGE BASKETBALL NAMES & GAMES

ORDER FORM
(please copy)

Credit Card orders
CALL TOLL FREE
1-800-544-6959
Visa and MasterCard
accepted

Mail to:
McClanahan Publishing House
P.O. Box 100
Kuttawa, KY   42055

Please send me_____copies of

     KY NAMES & GAMES @ $15.95   ————
     KY residents add .96¢ each   ————
     Postage/Handling $3.00
         plus .50¢ ea. additional book _____

                   TOTAL _____

Make check payable to:
McClanahan Publishing House

Ship to:

name_____

address_____

city_____st._____zip_____